The
Festivus
Haggadah

by

Martin Bodek

Also by Martin Bodek

The New Old Testament: Bush II, Book I

The Year of Bad Behavior: Bearing Witness to the Uncouthiest of Humanity

A Conversation on the Way

54 Runners, 54 Stories: The Tale of the JRunners 2012 200k Relay Race

Extracts from Noah's Diary

The Emoji Haggadah

The Festivus Haggadah

By Martin Bodek

Copyright © 2020 by Martin Bodek

Cover art by Elizabeth Ehrenpreis

Cover design by Elizabeth Ehrenpreis.

This book is a work of fictional non-fiction, or non-fictional fiction. We can't really tell. The characters, incidents, and dialogues are not products of the author's imagination and are to be construed as real. Well, in the sense that the Passover history happened, and the fictional history happened in the real TV world too. Following so far? Any resemblance to actual events or persons, living or dead, is not coincidental at all. They really happened, fictionally, and non-fictionally, as this book is a fusion. You know what, this is too confusing. Enjoy the ISBN number, and move on.

ISBN: 978-1-67811-365-0

For my sister, Devorah

The real Bee Movie

Table of Contents

You'll be Pleased to See What's Inside[1]

---

[1] S07E04, "The Wink," written by Tom Gammill, Max Pross.

Acknowledgements

Thank You Very Much Indeed[2]

Okay, deep breath, aaaaaaaand thank you to:

My Creator, for granting me a sense of humor, a probing mind, an appreciation for pop culture, and a desire to write books. With this book, these worlds are colliding.[3]

My wife Naomi, for everything, past, present, and future, and for being everything to everyone, and being my everything.

My daughter Naava, for being the apple of your mother's eye, and for taking on more responsibilities with grace and positivity.

My son Freddy, for owning worlds of promise, being my fellow Yankees/Giants fan, and partnering with me on our bar mitzvah reading.

My son Ranan, for your fearlessness, your capture-the-momentism, and your unbridled joy and enthusiasm.

My six folks – my mom Chantze, my aba Chaim, my dad Barry, my stepmom Leah, my MIL Rochelle, and my FIL Leon - for combining your efforts to mold me into what I've become: mostly a grateful person.

My sisters – Chanalah and Chaiy Bodek, Sara Shuman, and Devorah Wicentowsky – for your love, support, and encouragement. Devorah is this book's dedicatee, for about seven double-entendre reasons. One point for each reason you figure out.

Friends who express confidence in me and/or show interest in my work/buy every book I write/like every one of my Facebook publishing posts: Michael Szpilzinger, Doodie Miller, Darryl Singh, Stephen Schwartz, Chesky Rand, Ditza Katz, Ross Tabisel, Rav Pinky Schmeckelstein, Shia Itzkowitz, Sandy Eller, Eli Friedman, Jonathan Pittinsky, Avry Weinstein, Jack Engelberg, Jamey Kohn.

My nachas-in-laws, Mordechai & Tova Ovits, for their continued inspiration in intelligence, skill, commitment, and parenting.

David Adler – still, as ever, always, and eternally - my cornerman, cheerleader, and number one fan.

My British family – always hospitable and asking about my sales, progress, and writing career. This is flattering, motivating, and gratifying. Thanks Uncle Michael, Auntie Sue, Eytan, Aron & Ilana,

---

[2] S05E04, "The Sniffing Accountant," written by Larry David, Jerry Seinfeld.
[3] S07E08, "The Pool Guy," written by David Mandel.

Aliza & Simon, and Joel & Avital Storfer. Thank you Uncle Sooty, Auntie Hazel, Benjy & Laura, Jeremy & Jess, David and Jonny Israel.

Those who gave me a chance: Shloime Drillick, Rav Mordechai Finkelman, Binyamin Jolkovsky, Tzvi Mauer, Danny Levine.

Writers who pointed me in the right direction and/or have given me a few moments of their time and/or vowed to appear at my first book reading, may this happen speedily in our days, amen: Anna Olswanger, Marnie Winston-MacAuley, Rabbi Cary Friedman, Mark Levinson, Jonathan Tropper, David Bader, Joel Chasnoff, Jon Stewart, Lisa Alcalay Klug, Algonquin Jones, Shulem Deen, A.J. Jacobs.

Generous providers of assistance, encouragement, inspiration, guidance, counsel, and pavement-pounding with my books: My hockey guys, Marc H. Simon, David Adler, Chesky Rosenblum, Matt Katz, Steven Friedman, Steven Holmbraker, Yaakov Bressler, Yaakov Ochs, Meir Kruter, Mo Sanders, Baal Habos, Shia Itzkowitz, Sruli Derdik, Sandy Eller, Marnie Winston-MacAuley, Yossie Davis, Dov Kramer, Yaakov Sash, Bettina & Rebekka & Sarra Laskin, Doron Storfer, Arnon Storfer, Michal Alatin, Josh Weinstein, Dan Shuman, Niko Pfund, Ada Brunstein, Deborah Shor, Rabbi Yaakov Glasser.

My Cover Art/Content Sounding Boarders, who give excellent constructive criticism: Dena Szpilzinger, Yiddy Lebovits, Tova Ovits, Alon Stempel, Sandy Eller, Chesky Rand, Dina Vinar, Jodi Goldberg, Shia Itzkowitz, Avi Lew, Malky Tannenbaum Haimoff, Meir Kruter, Chaim Howard Nath, Dan Shuman, Michael Szpilzinger, Viva La Jewpacabra, Mitchell Silk, Chanan Feldman, Joel Mandel, Moshe Lewis, Rachel Warshower, Azi Steiner, David Schlachter, Avi Koplowitz, Shmuly Engelman, Ari Benscher, Benjamin Lieberman, Peretz Stern, Tzvi Jungreis, Fred MacDowell, Michael Appel, Yonah Wolf, David Friedman, Yossi Sharf, Elizabeth Ehrenpreis.

Jeff Goodstein – no single person has ever done more to improve the quality of any of my books. It started with my Noah book, but became perpetual. Your input continues to be invaluable.

Moishey Sharf – My on-staff eagle-eye pedantic Volunteer Editor, always available to help, but somehow missing the Oxford Commas I omit. All remaining typos are your fault. Kidding.

Anyone, who ever in my life gave me my favorite compliment: "Hey Bodek, you're a funny guy, you should write a book." Thank you so much, and look at me. I did. Yet again. For the seventh time.

Aaaaaand exhale.

Introduction

Or, Please Don't Send Jackie Chiles[4] After Me

My opening monologue

The query letter that I fashioned for this book, read, in part: "…a tribute, an homage, a comedic fusion of the classic haggadah template that fuses as much of the Seinfeld canon—and particularly, the curious details of the Festivus holiday—as possible into it…"

I mention this for three reasons:

1) I want you, who picked up this book, to have a proper feel for what it's all about. I think the concise statement above nails it. You know what you have in hand, you know you want it, and you're gonna need it.[5]

2) I want the Seinfeld creators to know that I'm simply a fan, that I come in peace and love, that the "tribute" and "homage" statements are serious, that this should help to pad their bottom line, and that my sentiment covers the same ground in Dave Cowen's "Yada Yada Haggadah," which is that this is a parody, protected by the laws of fair use, transforms the copyrighted material into a teaching tool for Judaism, won't have a negative effect on the market for the show,[6] and will have a positive impact on Mr. Cowen's funny books. I also endeavored mightily to give proper credit to every writer of every episode, on the page of citation itself, for maxim viewability and credit. You can see in these first few pages that I've already begun to do that.

3) I'm proud of the concise statement. I spent an inordinate amount of time perfecting it, got good feedback for it, and grabbed the attention of the first publisher I queried. Not the third, not the second, the first. This is my way of patting myself on the back.

---

[4] First appearance: S07E03, "The Maestro," written by Larry David.

[5] S03E14, "The Pez Dispenser," written by Larry David.

[6] Introduction, "The Yada Yada Haggadah: A Sitcom Seder," written by Dave Cowen.

How this book came to be

Coming off the personally-unprecedented[7] success of "The Emoji Haggadah" – which sold thousands more than anything I'd previously published, got more press than I could ever imagine, and wound up in stores and libraries I'd only ever dreamed of having a book in – I had to think hard about my follow-up.

My first idea was to write "The Emoji x," whatever "x" might be. I polled Facebook and got good feedback for a potential "sequel."

But!

My wife, Naomi, and my good man Yaakov Sash, both advised that "The Emoji x" was not the next idea, and never should be, because "The Emoji Haggadah" was already the most practical Jewish-book emoji idea possible, and any other idea would fail in comparison, and pale in practical use, to the original.

No, it would be wiser to write "The x Haggadah," because the haggadah lends itself to flexibility, malleability, usability, and creativity. My sequel should be the next idea along these lines.

Now, annually, I post a "book report" to my blog and to Facebook, in which I detail how my books are doing, how books in the pipeline are faring, and ideas in my head not yet committed to paper. One of these in the latter category was "The Festivus Haggadah." The holiday is still in its nascent phase, waiting for something to tip it into the wider culture. I always figured a proper text, a formalization of sorts, would be that tipping point.

I decided to take the pen, go ahead, [8] put it to paper, see what happens.

Phase I: the easy stuff

At the outset, I already knew that I'd be squeezing blood from a stone. The total Festivus airtime is under five minutes, and I couldn't squish a whole book out of it, could I? However, I knew that if I got off to a good, creative start with the easy stuff, I'd be motivated to continue, and I'd find a way to slog through the hard stuff.

---

[7] S05E20, "The Fire," written by Larry Charles.
[8] S03E03, "The Pen," written by Larry David.

First up was the Four Questions, easiest of all. I simply take all the Festivus minutiae, and ask questions about it. Easy peasy. I immediately stretched it to six, and later to eight, and resolved to double or treble all such numbered things, because that's funny.

Next up was the Four Sons, which followed the template above. Four was easy, then stretched it further, and wound up with eight. I could have gone much further, but too much isn't funny. Following this pattern, I then doubled the ten plagues.

"Dayenu" was next, the biggest softball of all, and written in ten minutes. You can easily see how I built that out. It was like buttah.

At this point, I started reaching out to friends and formed my Sounding Board Committee. I got lots of good ideas, especially from Yossi Sharf and Jeff Goodstein, who helped me formulate some jokes and some directions for the seder.

Next up was "Echad Mi Yodaya?" My first thought was, "Could I find Seinfeld numbers up to 13? Waitasec, why stop at 13? How many numbers further could I get? If I go further, should it follow the way the haggadah does it? Restart with every number? Wouldn't that make the book about the size of a Dumas or Hugo classic?

I googled a bit, and found whole sites dedicated to Seinfeld's numbers. I also found a bajillion[9] Sporcle quizzes, many focusing on just numbers. I then found a book called "Seinfeld FAQ," by Nicholas Nigro, which contained numbers galore. I realized that all this is not enough. I'll get lots of data from these methods, but I might be missing stuff, so I began binge-watching the entire series. I also lent from NYPL both notable extant Festivus books, "Festivus! The Book," by Mark Nelson and "Festivus: The Holiday for the Rest of Us," by Allen Salkin. I got to a crazy number, as you'll see, and created an unreal, gargantuan spreadsheet. I'm looking at it now. Sweet Fancy Moses.[10]

The final piece of my first stab was "Chad Gadya." I stressed over this for days while continuing to fill out some easy parts (Next Year, Bitter herbs, and the decision to use Ovaltine as a stand-in for wine), but it hit me: the pilot! From where it all started! Just like the song! I looked up Seinfeld's history, browsed the episode list, took count of all its awards, and badabing, the book skeleton was complete.

---

[9] Autocorrect should realize this is a legitimate word.
[10] S08E04, "The Little Kicks," written by Spike Feresten.

Phase II: clustering and categorizing

Skeletons are nice, but some flesh is better. The first section I looked at as rather bland was The Sixteen Persons (when it was merely eight). Something was missing. Many of the Sporcle quizzes contained character nicknames, and there was a world of them. I figured, hey, why narrow the characters down to a single sobriquet. Why not list them all? So that's what I did. And that section positively exploded. As I binge-watched, I continued filling in what googling missed.

I then realized, upon running out of Festivus/Haggadah fusion material that I needed pages dedicated to Newman, Kramer's inventions, and Jerry, George, and Elaine's numerous ill-fated relationships. Newman's page came to me first, and like Improv, once you get a great idea, punchlines flow. Jerry was next, I had to catalogue how his girlfriends broke up with him, not the other way around, because comeuppance is funny. I then found the right section, as you'll see.

Kramer's invention section was much harder, and required a lot of brainstorming. I kept scrolling through the manuscript, looking for the right place. Once I contemplated that inventions are a way of asking a question and filling a void, I finally found it. It was a bit of a stretch, but I think you'll enjoy the results.

Once that was complete, I had trouble figuring out where to insert George's breakups. Again, I stretched it just a bit, but found it rather fitting.

Almost finally, I needed a spot for the leftover insults, sobriquets, and human appelations. I found that in "Avodim Hayinu."

Finally, "Shulchan Orech" was an idea that hit me in the head like a falling air conditioner.[11] I couldn't just write "Eat and drink." That's boring. No, I had to include what you shouldn't do when you eat and drink, and the Seinfeld series is positively filled to overspilling with those faux pas.[12]

As I continued binge-watching, I kept filling out all the above sections, and they kept bleeding over into the next page, enlarging the manuscript to my satisfaction, and hopefully, to yours.

---

[11] S08E04, "The Little Kicks," written by Spike Feresten.
[12] Fauxs pa?

Phase III: epiphanies and the hard stuff

Now it was time to address the hard stuff. Who is the book saying prayers to? It's supposed to be irreligious, so who is the deity the text is thanking?

See, I was committed to (pinkish) hewing[13] to the haggadah framework, because that would be funny, but it was giving me problems. I then hit upon Frank as the deity, because worshiping him would be both a religious and irreligious move.

But a great heap of the haggadah is endless praise. How was I to address those? I decided to employ a limited set of "Yada yada"s.

The rest was major brain work. I had to reinvent the songs at the end of the haggadah from scratch. These weren't easy, but I think I acquitted myself nicely.

The final piece of the puzzle was my commitment to footnote every single Seinfeld episode. All 180. Because that would be funny, and I'm crazy.

When I was done with the entire text, I then quality-controlled the footnotes to check if I had gotten them all. I was missing just five, but after viewing them during my marathon binge-watch, I found elements to include in the text.

Alas, throughout all the writing, I could not figure out a way to include Elaine's boyfriends into the text.

That's a shame.

My closing monologue

And I was done, and there's a lot more to be said about my joke-writing process, but a magician can't reveal all his tricks, and I needed to write all this down so I could reference it for media interviews, and this introduction is now five pages long, but it's over, and I did it the fun way,[14] and now you have a book to read.

Enjoy!

Or, taste the fruits and let the juices drip down your chin.[15]

---

[13] S03E16, "The Fix-Up," written by Larry Charles, Elaine Pope.
[14] S08E19, "The Yada Yada," written by Peter Mehlman, Jill Franklin.
[15] S05E10, "The Summer of George," written by Alec Berg & Jeff Schaffer.

The
Festivus
Haggadah

Blessings

Or, The Airing of Pleasantries[16]

Go.

All present dress in their finest cabana wear,[17] while the gentlemen of the household don their puffy shirts.[18] We pour the first cup of Ovaltine,[19] or Snapple, if it is not too fruity.[20] The marble ryes[21] are covered.

We make the blessings to open the Seder. Note: soup is not a seder.[22]

On non-denominational religious days honoring the deity of your choice – which is your business; not that there is anything wrong with that[23] - begin here:

> And there was evening and there was morning, the twenty-fifth day. And the fathers were finished with their fighting over that doll (she was very special), and all their host. And on that day Frank finished contemplating this fighting which He had done; and He resolved on that day from all this fighting, and He realized there must be another way. And Frank mundaned the day two days prior,[24] and desacralized it; because He declared Festivus upon it for the rest of us, throughout the generations.[25]

---

[16] S09E10, "The Strike," written by Dan O'Keefe, Alec Berg, Jeff Schaffer.

[17] S05E18/19, "The Raincoats," written by Tom Gammill, Max Pross, Larry David, Jerry Seinfeld.

[18] S05E02, "The Puffy Shirt," written by Larry David.

[19] S08E06, "The Fatigues," written by Gregg Kavet, Andy Robin.

[20] S04E15, "The Visa," written by Peter Mehlman.

[21] S07E11, "The Rye," written by Carol Leifer.

[22] S06E07, "The Soup," written by Fred Stoller.

[23] S04E17, "The Outing," written by Larry Charles.

[24] In the O'Keefe household, Festivus was random, and sometimes twice a year, but has formally been celebrated on 12/23 in the wider culture.

[25] S09E10, "The Strike," written by Dan O'Keefe, Alec Berg, Jeff Schaffer.

On days lacking Alternate Side,[26] begin here:

> Blessed are you, Frank our Founder, Master of His Household, who creates the Festivus holiday.

> Blessed are You, Frank our Founder, Master of His Household, who has chosen us from all peoples and has raised us above all tongues and has desacralized us with His silly rituals. And You have given us, Frank our Founder, an appointed time for happiness, a holiday and a special time for joy, this Festival of Festivus, our season of freedom, a profane convocation in memory of the exodus from commercialism and religion. For You have chosen us and desacralized us above all peoples. In Your gracious love, You granted us Your special time for happiness and joy.

> Blessed are You, O Frank, who desacralizes the people, and the appointed time.

On the cessation of the non-denominational holiday of your choice, add the following two paragraphs:

> Blessed are You, Frank our Founder, Master of His Household, who creates the manssiere of the man.[27] Blessed are You, Frank our Founder, Master of His Household, who distinguishes between the profane and the nonclerical, between the bro and the manssiere, between regular clothes and cabana wear,[28] between the pool house and the shuffleboard court.[29] You have distinguished between the irreverence of the non-denominational holiday of your choice and the irreverence of the Festivus Festival, and You have desacralized the non-denominational holiday of your choice above the previous working days of your choice.

---

[26] S03E11, "The Alternate Side," written by Larry David, Bill Masters.

[27] S06E18, "The Doorman," written by Tom Gammill, Max Pross.

[28] S05E18/19, "The Raincoats," written by Tom Gammill, Max Pross, Larry David, Jerry Seinfeld.

[29] S07E16, "The Shower Head," written by Peter Mehlman, Marjorie Gross.

You have distinguished and desacralized Your people with Your irreverence.

Blessed are You, O Frank, who distinguishes between the normal human speech and a strange halting way of speaking.[30]

Blessed are You, Frank our Founder, Master of His Household, who has granted us joy and silliness and guided us to reach this season.

Drink while reclining to the left and do not recite a blessing after drinking.

Some say you raise the feet, get blood to the head. Others say you raise the head, you get blood to the feet.[31]

---

[30] S06E24, "The Understudy," written by Marjorie Gross, Carol Leifer.
[31] S03E11, "The Alternate Side," written by Larry David, Bill Masters.

Washing

With Commando 450 Pressure[32]

Wash your hands (because the head of the household will not tolerate infestation)[33] but do not say the blessing "on the washing of the hands."

In some communities, only the head of the household washes his hands. Finicky guests are welcome to join.[34]

While you are waiting for them to come back, feel free to discuss these things amongst your dinnermates:

Is it a marble rye when it comes out of the oven? Or the moment you put your fists in the dough?[35]

Or, if your brain is so mossy that you percolate an idea to open a restaurant that serves only peanut butter and jelly sandwiches, do you need more sleep?[36]

Or, if you're in a restaurant, with a big meeting coming up, and you get mustard on your tie, wouldn't a dispenser that rolls out new ties come in real handy?[37]

Or, if you test a giant rubber ball of oil's integrity onto a busy street, are you crazy – to abandon the idea after one try?[38]

Or, how about this: would you be interested in ketchup and mustard in the same bottle?[39]

---

[32] S07E16, "The Shower Head," written by Peter Mehlman, Marjorie Gross.

[33] S05E18/19, "The Raincoats," written by Tom Gammill, Max Pross, Larry David, Jerry Seinfeld.

[34] S05E15, "The Pie," written by Tom Gammill, Max Pross.

[35] S06E05, "The Couch," written by Larry David.

[36] S07E18, "The Friar's Club," written by David Mandel.

[37] S01E05, "The Stock Tip," written by Larry David, Jerry Seinfeld.

[38] S09E02, "The Voice," written by Alec Berg, Jeff Schaffer, David Mandel.

[39] Ibid.

Or, how you gonna drive when looking through a periscope?[40]

Or, if you scald yourself with a café latte, and they put the top on, you didn't put the top in, with a top they made, because you didn't make the top, and you sue, because this is outrageous, egregious, preposterous, and meet with the company owners, who offer you "all the free coffee you want in any of their stores throughout North America and Europe, plus," do you take it, or do you want to hear what comes after "plus."[41]

Or, while you're at it, if you chain-smoke yourself into hideousness, sallowness, unattractiveness, disgustingness, horrible twisted freakiness, gobliness, shrunken headedness, and wretched disfigurement, would you settle for a poster of your rugged masculinity in Times Square?[42]

Or, if the bra don't fit, must you acquit?[43]

Or, who would like a coffee table book about coffee tables that turns into a coffee table, for your coffee table?[44]

Or, what sounds more logical, a beltless trench coat, or a brimless rain-hat?[45]

Or, if you're a, shall we say, gynecomaster of your domain, would you like a support undergarment to fasten with Velcro or a hook?[46]

Or, if you were Miss America, what would you do to make the world a better place? What advice would you give young people? What's your talent? How's your evening? If you were Miss America, and the U.S. was on the brink of a nuclear war, and the only way the conflict could be averted was if you agreed to sleep with the enemy's leader, what would you do? How ya feelin'?[47]

---

[40] S07E24, "The Invitations," written by Larry David.
[41] S07E03, "The Maestro," written by Larry David.
[42] S08E09, "The Abstinence," written by Steve Koren.
[43] S07E12, "The Caddy," written by Gregg Kavet, Andy Robin.
[44] S05E22, "The Opposite," written by Andy Cowan, Larry David, Jerry Seinfeld.
[45] S05E18/19, "The Raincoats," written by Tom Gammill, Max Pross, Larry David, Jerry Seinfeld.
[46] S06E18, "The Doorman," written by Tom Gammill, Max Pross.
[47] S06E01, "The Chaperone," written by Larry David, Bill Masters, Bob Shaw.

Or, is it really that difficult to let someone go from a job he doesn't actually have?[48]

Or, would you engage in criminal behavior that's only illegal in America?[49]

Or, are Dominicans Cubans?[50]

Or, for how much money would you sell the suit right off your body?[51]

Or, for how much money would you sell your life stories, if you were never allowed to tell them again?[52]

Or, would you pay $37.50 for a Bite Sized Three Musketeers?[53]

Or, if a New York bottle deposit is 5 cents, and is 10 cents in Michigan, and transport is too expensive, and overhead is too high, what kind of truck would be needed, on what kind of day, to lower the variable and fixed costs of redemption to zero?[54]

Or, if you put Japanese businessman to bed in a chest of drawers, would it create an international incident?[55]

Or, if you can't peel, chop, grate, or mince, and have no sense of flavor, and can't multiply 4-6 people to get to 183 peole, and dropped the kreplach, and left the stuffed cabbage in the elevator, and are not Jewish, should you also be trying to make the tsimmis, brisket, and kugel for a Jewish Singles Event?[56]

Or, are "Hey," "How you doin'?," What's happening?," "What's up?," or How's it going?" the same as "Hello?" Would $20 convince you that they are?[57]

---

[48] S08E03, "The Bizarro Jerry," written by David Mandel.

[49] S08E11, "The Little Jerry," written by Jennifer Crittenden.

[50] S08E17, "The English Patient," written by Steve Koren.

[51] S06E09, "The Secretary," written by Carol Leifer, Marjorie Gross.

[52] S08E14, "The Van Buren Boys," written by Darin Henry.

[53] S08E21, "The Muffin Tops," written by Spike Feresten.

[54] S07E21/22, "The Bottle Deposit," written by Gregg Kavet, Andy Robin.

[55] S08E07, "The Checks," written by Steve O'Donnell, Tom Gammill, Max Pross.

[56] S08E06, "The Fatigues," written by Gregg Kavet, Andy Robin.

[57] S07E24, "The Invitations," written by Larry David.

Or, if you find yourself betting on airplane arrivals and departures, and a friend is responsible for a delay, have you cheated?[58]

Or, does the city need more slow moving wicker vehicles? If so, would the physically fit homeless – with well-toned upper bodies, or a shirt - be ideal drivers due to their intimate knowledge of the street?[59]

Or, if given a choice of fake diseases, would you go with severe pain, nausea, and delusions, or burning during urination and the haunting memories of lost love?[60]

Or, if you're invited to a fake talk show set up inside a friend's apartment, should you admit to criminal activity, or bring prey where predators will be present?[61]

Or, if one were to create a pasta statue of your likeness, which one would capture your individuality?[62]

Or, do you think people are going to pay $80 a bottle to smell like dead fish and seaweed?[63]

I can't believe I'm saying this: that's not a bad idea.

Actually, it's pretyyyyyy pretyyyyyy good.[64]

---

[58] S06E22, "The Diplomat's Club," written by Tom Gammill, Max Pross.

[59] S09E17, "The Bookstore," written by Spike Feresten, Darin Henry, Marc Jaffe.

[60] S09E16, "The Burning," written by Jennifer Crittenden.

[61] S09E06, "The Merv Griffin Show," written by Bruce Eric Kaplan.

[62] S06E21, "The Fusilli Jerry," written by Marjorie Gross, Jonathan Gross, Ron Hauge, Charlie Rubin.

[63] S03E14, "The Pez Dispenser," written by Larry David.

[64] There was no way I wasn't going to put in a Curb Your Enthusiasm reference.

Greens

Such as Cramp Bark, Cleavers, and Couch Grass[65]

Take from the greens less than a Mackinaw peach's[66] measure - so that you will not need to say the blessing after eating it; dip it into the cold water; say the blessing "Who creates the Festivus upon which to eat the fruit of the earth;" and have in mind that this blessing will also be for the bitter herbs.[67] Eat without reclining.

> Blessed are you, Frank our Founder, Master of His Household, Who creates the Festivus upon which to eat the fruit of the earth.

One might think that this small measure is not all that it could be, when in fact, it is all that it *should* be, and more![68]

But it's not like after the risotto.[69]

---

[65] S02E08, "The Heart Attack," written by Larry Charles.

[66] S06E20, "The Doodle," written by Alec Berg, Jeff Schaffer.

[67] A metaphor for the Airing of Grievances, duh.

[68] S05E21, "The Hamptons," written by Peter Mehlman, Carol Leifer.

[69] S05E01, "The Mango," written by Lawrence H. Levy, Larry David.

Break-up

Like a Band Aid. One Motion. Right Off![70]

Split the greens in two and reshuffle the contents. Place the small salad back on the table, and conceal the Big Salad[71] to use it for the afikavorkah,[72] [73] which children customarily steal, because they wanna be a pirate.[74]

While we are separating things, if you have a boyfriend who thinks you are two-faced, now would be a great time to break up with him.[75]

Or if you believe you caught him with a pick that was clearly not on the outside.[76]

Or if he shares with his friends that you like a commercial that he does not like.[77]

Or if he cannot remember your name, despite that it rhymes with a female body part.[78]

Or if he imagines with his friends that your stomach talks in a funny voice after you fall asleep, then chooses the voice over you.[79]

Or if he is a bit too nosy about why you always wear the same dress.[80]

Or if you made a bad decision on a stock, and refusing to tell him which perfume you are wearing is not enough.[81]

---

[70] S02E01, "The Ex-Girlfriend," written by Larry David, Jerry Seinfeld.
[71] S06E02, "The Big Salad," written by Larry David.
[72] S05E11, "The Conversion," written by Bruce Kirschbaum.
[73] From the Greek Latvian Orthodox, which means "dessert lure of the animal."
[74] S05E02, "The Puffy Shirt," written by Larry David.
[75] S09E10, "The Strike," written by Dan O'Keefe, Alec Berg, Jeff Schaffer.
[76] S04E13, "The Pick," written by Larry David, Marc Jaffe.
[77] S02E04, "The Phone Message," written by Larry David, Jerry Seinfeld.
[78] S04E20, "The Junior Mint," written by Andy Robin.
[79] S09E02, "The Voice," written by Alec Berg, Jeff Schaffer, David Mandel.
[80] S07E13, "The Seven," written by Alec Berg, Jeff Schaffer.
[81] S01E05, "The Stock Tip," written by Larry David, Jerry Seinfeld.

Or if he asks if your panties were laid out by your mother.[82]

Or if he is thin, single, and neat. Not that there is anything wrong with that.[83]

Of if he made way too many cultural puns at your expense.[84]

Or if he dispatched a friend to determine whether or not they are real.[85]

Or if is this same friend will not spare a square.[86]

Or if he hides meat inside your grandmother's heirloom napkins.[87]

Or if he refuses to kiss you on the grounds that you previously dated an enemy of his who broke up with you because you were not pretty enough.[88]

Or if he thinks you have a laugh that is like Elmer Fudd sitting on a juicer.[89]

Or if he gives his 25% dry cleaners discount to another fake wife.[90]

Or if he is too nosy about you wearing the same dress all the time.[91]

Or if you will not submit to forcible massage.[92]

Or if he tells jokes, but is no comedian.[93]

Or if you have a crush on his next door neighbor.[94]

Or if his protégé is a hack.[95]

---

[82] S04E08, "The Cheever Letters," written by Larry David, Elaine Pope, Tom Leopold.
[83] S04E17, "The Outing," written by Larry Charles.
[84] S05E10, "The Cigar Store Indian," written by Tom Gammill, Max Pross.
[85] S04E19, "The Implant," written by Peter Mehlman.
[86] S05E12, "The Stall," written by Larry Charles.
[87] S07E04, "The Wink," written by Tom Gammill, Max Pross.
[88] S06E02, "The Big Salad," written by Larry David.
[89] S04E07, "The Bubble Boy," written by Larry David, Larry Charles.
[90] S05E17, "The Wife," written by Peter Mehlman.
[91] S07E13, "The Seven," written by Alec Berg, Jeff Schaffer.
[92] S05E09, "The Masseuse," written by Peter Mehlman.
[93] S06E06, "The Gymnast," written by Alec Berg, Jeff Schaffer.
[94] S08E02, "The Soul Mate," written by Peter Mehlman.
[95] S08E06, "The Fatigues," written by Gregg Kavet, Andy Robin.

Of if he insults your profession because it doesn't save lives, when in fact, it does.[96]

Or if he refused to pay you for cleaning his place, even though there was not much cleaning going on.[97]

Or if you do not like his act.[98]

Or if he got too angry after you encouraged him to get angry.[99]

Or if you suddenly mutually realize that you both hate each other.[100]

Or if he drugged you so he could play with your toys.[101]

Or if he raided your medicine cabinet.[102]

Or if he participated in a contest.[103]

---

[96] S09E07, "The Slicer," written by Gregg Kavet, Andy Robin, Darin Henry.
[97] S09E19, "The Maid," written by Alec Berg, David Mandel, Jeff Schaffer, Kit Boss, Peter Mehlman.
[98] S02E01, "The Ex-Girlfriend," written by Larry David, Jerry Seinfeld.
[99] S09E03, "The Serenity Now," written by Steve Koren.
[100] S08E01, "The Foundation," written by Alec Berg, Jeff Schaffer.
[101] S09E06, "The Merv Griffin Show," written by Bruce Eric Kaplan.
[102] S05E11, "The Conversion," written by Bruce Kirschbaum.
[103] S04E11, "The Contest," written by Larry David.

Recitation
Of the Miracles of Festivus

The Meatloaf[104] of Destitution

Hey, Salad's Got Nuttin' on this Mutton[105]

The head of household uncovers the meatloaf, raises the seder plate, and says out loud:

> This is the meatloaf of destitution that our ancestors ate in the neighborhood of Bayside. Anyone who is famished should come and eat, anyone who is in need should come and partake of the Festivus sacrifice. If you have a reservation, we know how to hold your reser[106] - uh, arrange for the appropriate accommodation.[107] Now we are here, next year we will be in Del Boca Vista; this year we are slaves, next year we will be out there, and lovin' every minute of it.[108]

---

[104] Real name: Marvin Lee Aday.

[105] S07E04, "The Wink," written by Tom Gammill, Max Pross.

[106] S03E11, "The Alternate Side," written by Larry David, Bill Masters.

[107] S05E10, "The Cigar Store Indian," written by Tom Gammill, Max Pross.

[108] S06E04, "The Chinese Woman," written by Peter Mehlman.

The Eight Questions

Though We Could Have Done a Lot More than This[109]

The head of household removes the seder plate from the table. We pour a second cup of Ovaltine, or Hennigan's no-smell no-tell Scotch.[110] The youngest child then asks:

What differentiates this night from all other nights?

1) On all other nights we eat chicken and meatloaf; tonight, only meatloaf.
2) On all other nights we eat other vegetables; tonight only peas and mashed potatoes.
3) On all other nights, we do not dip our food, even one time; tonight we double dip (once in lettuce, and once in paella).[111]
4) On all other nights, we eat either sitting or reclining; tonight we all recline in each other's faces as we air grievances.
5) On all other nights, we give of our tithes to various entities; tonight we give only to The Human Fund.
6) On all other nights, we have decorations of all kinds; tonight we only have a pole, with no tinsel. Too distracting.
7) On all other nights, we discourse on our tragedies and miracles; tonight we relay only our Festivus miracles.
8) On all other nights, we have Festivus No, Bagels Yes. Tonight we have Festivus Yes, Bagels No.

---

[109] S07E23, "The Wait Out," written by Peter Mehlman, Matt Selman.
[110] S03E12, "The Red Dot," written by Larry David.
[111] S05E18/19, "The Raincoats," written by Tom Gammill, Max Pross, Larry David, Jerry Seinfeld.

We Were Subjugated in Bayside

Say, Does Butlering Jerry[112] Violate the 13th Amendment?[113]

The head of household puts the seder plate back on the table. The meatloaf should be uncovered during The Recitation portion of the Haggadah.

> We were slaves to our corporate and religious overlords in the neighborhood of Bayside, and Frank, our Founder, took us out from there with a strong hand and an outstretched forearm. Namely, Feats of Strength. And if The Frank One, blessed be He, had not taken our ancestors out from monopolizing business and religion behemoths, behold we and our children and our children's children would all be subjugated to conglomerates in Bayside. And even if we were all sages, all discerning, all elders, all knowledgeable about the non-sectarian book of scripture of your choice, it would be a commandment upon us to tell the story of the exodus from commercialism and religion. And anyone who adds - and spends extra time - in telling the story of the exodus, behold he is praiseworthy.
>
> And anyone who does not, is a rabid anti-dentite.[114]
>
> Or at least a Moop.[115]
>
> Who is not artistic and has no integrity.[116]
>
> And contributes nothing to society.[117]

---

[112] S04E23/24, "The Pilot," written by Larry David.

[113] "Neither slavery nor involuntary servitude, except as a punishment for crime whereof the party shall have been duly convicted, shall exist within the United States, or any place subject to their jurisdiction."

[114] S08E19, "The Yada Yada," written by Peter Mehlman, Jill Franklin.

[115] S04E07, "The Bubble Boy," written by Larry David, Larry Charles.

[116] S04E03, "The Pitch," written by Larry David.

[117] S03E04, "The Dog," written by Larry David.

Certainly, at minimum, an unspongeworthy,[118] man-handed,[119] re-gifting,[120] de-gifting,[121] close-talking,[122] not-loud-talking-but-high-talking,[123] long-talking,[124] pie-refusing,[125] naked coughing,[126] Kiss Hello-shunning,[127] caveman-armed,[128] pinheaded,[129] step-skipping,[130] stink-eyed,[131] crook-eyed,[132] evil-eyed,[133] toe-thumbed,[134] head-first parking[135] name-naming,[136] Peter Pan-complexed,[137] Downtown-numbered,[138] pigmannish,[139] mimboesque,[140] sidlering,[141] Vegetable Lasagnaed,[142] Pimple-popper, M.D.ed,[143] Bad break-upping,[144] sentence-finishing,[145] Cell phone walk-and-

[118] S07E09, "The Sponge," written by Peter Mehlman.
[119] S08E03, "The Bizarro Jerry," written by David Mandel.
[120] S06E12, "The Label Maker," written by Alec Berg, Jeff Schaffer.
[121] Ibid.
[122] S05E18/19, "The Raincoats," written by Tom Gammill, Max Pross, Larry David, Jerry Seinfeld.
[123] S06E03, "The Pledge Drive," written by Tom Gammill, Max Pross.
[124] S06E04, "The Chinese Woman," written by Peter Mehlman.
[125] S05E15, "The Pie," written by Tom Gammill, Max Pross.
[126] S09E09, "The Apology," written by Jennifer Crittenden.
[127] S06E17, "The Kiss Hello," written by Larry David, Jerry Seinfeld.
[128] S05E10, "The Summer of George," written by Alec Berg & Jeff Schaffer.
[129] S09E09, "The Apology," written by Jennifer Crittenden.
[130] Ibid.
[131] S08E14, "The Van Buren Boys," written by Darin Henry.
[132] Ibid.
[133] S09E08, "The Betrayal," written by David Mandel, Peter Mehlman.
[134] S09E16, "The Burning," written by Jennifer Crittenden.
[135] S03E22, "The Parking Space," written by Larry David, Greg Daniels.
[136] S06E10, "The Race," written by Tom Gammill, Max Pross, Larry David, Sam Kass.
[137] S06E08, "The Mom & Pop Store," written by Tom Gammill, Max Pross.
[138] S09E19, "The Maid," written by Alec Berg, David Mandel, Jeff Schaffer, Kit Boss, Peter Mehlman.
[139] S05E05, "The Bris," written by Larry Charles.
[140] S05E12, "The Stall," written by Larry Charles.
[141] S09E06, "The Merv Griffin Show," written by Bruce Eric Kaplan.
[142] S09E01, "The Butter Shave," written by Alec Berg, Jeff Schaffer, David Mandel.
[143] S09E07, "The Slicer," written by Gregg Kavet, Andy Robin, Darin Henry.
[144] S08E10, "The Andrea Doria," written by Spike Feresten.
[145] S09E18, "The Frogger," written by Gregg Kavet, Andy Robin, Steve Koren, Dan O'Keefe.

talking[146] Mulva[147] with shrinkage,[148] whose (so-so)[149] sorries you can stuff in a sack, mister![150]

And is not as good looking as they think they are.[151]

Yeah, that's right.[152]

---

[146] S09E23/24, "The Finale," written by Larry David.

[147] S04E20, "The Junior Mint," written by Andy Robin.

[148] S05E21, "The Hamptons," written by Peter Mehlman, Carol Leifer.

[149] S03E22, "The Parking Space," written by Larry David, Greg Daniels.

[150] S09E08, "The Betrayal," written by David Mandel, Peter Mehlman.

[151] S04E21, "The Smelly Car," written by Larry David, Peter Mehlman.

[152] Almost as frequently cited as "That's a shame," and "Who is this?"

The Story of the Five Rabbis

None of Whom Babble Elaine's Secrets[153] or Renounce[154] for Her

It happened once on Festivus that Rabbi Simon, Rabbi Bennett, Rabbi Robbins, Rabbi Oppenheim, and Rabbi Taft[155] were reclining in New York and were telling the story of the exodus from commercialism and religion that whole night, until their students came and said to them, "The time of waking Jean-Paul has arrived."[156]

Rabbi Cosmo ben Babs[157] said, "Behold I am craggy and crinkly, for I have accomplished a lifetime of smoking in seventy-two hours,[158] and I have not merited to understand why the exodus from commercialism and religion should be said at night until Ben Daniel[159] explicated it, as it is stated (Costanzonomy 16:3), "In order that you remember the day of your going out from the straits of consumerism and faith all the days of your life;" "the days of your life" indicates that the remembrance be invoked during the days, "all the days of your life" indicates that the remembrance be invoked also during the nights." But the Sages say, "'the days of your life' indicates that the remembrance be invoked in this world, 'all the days of your life' indicates that the remembrance be invoked also in the days of the end-of-days savior of your choice."

---

153 S07E02, "The Postponement," written by Larry David.

154 S09E03, "The Serenity Now," written by Steve Koren.

155 S01E02, "The Stake Out," written by Larry David, Jerry Seinfeld.

156 S07E05, "The Hot Tub," written by Gregg Kavet, Andy Robin.

157 S06E11, "The Switch," written by Bruce Kirschbaum, Sam Kass.

158 S08E09, "The Abstinence," written by Steve Koren.

159 My wink and nod to the O'Keefe family, the original creators, participators, and chroniclers of Festivus. I'll pepper in a few more.

The Sixteen Persons[160]

This Does Not Necessarily[161] Cover all New York Stereotypes

Blessed be the Head of Household of all, blessed be He.

Blessed be the Frank who gave the non-sectarian scripture to His people, blessed be He.

Corresponding to sixteen persons did the non-sectarian scripture speak:

1) The Comedian,[162]
2) The Lord of the Idiots,[163]
3) The Hipster Doofus,[164]
4) The Shiksappealing,[165]
5) The Cashier,[166]
6) The Enigma, a Mystery Wrapped in a Riddle,[167]
7) The Boss,[168]
8) The Belligerent Patriarch,[169]
9) The Put-upon Team-Switching Fiancee,[170]
10) The Melodramatic Matriarch,[171]

---

[160] For giggles, I've listed characters by most appearances. Surprises aplenty.

[161] S09E08, "The Betrayal," written by David Mandel, Peter Mehlman.

[162] S06E06, "The Gymnast," written by Alec Berg, Jeff Schaffer.

[163] S02E05, "The Apartment," written by Peter Mehlman.

[164] S05E03, "The Glasses," written by Tom Gammill, Max Pross.

[165] S09E03, "The Serenity Now," written by Steve Koren.

[166] First appearance: S04E01/02, "The Trip," written by Larry Charles. First speaking lines: S07E10, "The Gum," written by Tom Gammill, Max Pross.

[167] S06E02, "The Big Salad," written by Larry David.

[168] First appearance: S05E22, "The Opposite," written by Andy Cowan, Larry David, Jerry Seinfeld.

[169] First played by John Randolph in S04E22, "The Handicap Spot," written by Larry David, and subsequently by Jerry Stiller.

[170] First appearance: S04E03, "The Pitch," written by Larry David.

[171] First appearance: S04E11, "The Contest," written by Larry David.

11) The Number-crunching Yiddishe Tatte,[172]
12) The Ever-doting Yiddishe Mamme,[173]
13) The Noir-Voiced World-traveling Adventurer,[174]
14) The Old Coot,[175]
15) The Forgetful Supervisor,[176]
16) and The Mimboyfriend.[177]

What does The Comedian[178] person – also known as Even Steven,[179] Terrorist Bomber,[180] Simple Man,[181] Clicker,[182] Claude,[183] Master Packer,[184] Stan,[185] Slappy White,[186] Professor High Brow,[187] Munjamba,[188] Funny Boy/Joy Boy/Junior/Punk,[189] (Big) Phony,[190] Bob,[191] Big Jerry/ Has Been,[192] The Devil,[193] Jerome,[194] Gillooly,[195] The Count of Monte Cristo/Pirate/Pirate

---

[172] First played by Phil Bruns in S01E02, "The Stake Out," written by Larry David, Jerry Seinfeld, and subsequently by Barney Martin.

[173] First appearance: S01E02, "The Stake Out," written by Larry David, Jerry Seinfeld

[174] First appearance: S06E24, "The Understudy," written by Marjorie Gross, Carol Leifer.

[175] First appearance: S02E02, "The Pony Remark," written by Larry David, Jerry Seinfeld.

[176] First appearance: S06E19, "The Jimmy," written by Gregg Kavet, Andy Robin.

[177] First appearance: S06E21, "The Fusilli Jerry," written by Marjorie Gross, Jonathan Gross, Ron Hauge, Charlie Rubin

[178] Jerry is the only character who appears in all of Seinfeld's 180 episodes.

[179] S05E22, "The Opposite," written by Andy Cowan, Larry David, Jerry Seinfeld.

[180] S08E18, "The Nap," written by Gregg Kavet, Andy Robin.

[181] S08E09, "The Abstinence," written by Steve Koren.

[182] S03E21, "The Letter," written by Larry David.

[183] S05E09, "The Masseuse," written by Peter Mehlman.

[184] S01E03, "The Robbery," written by Matt Goldman.

[185] S06E01, "The Chaperone," written by Larry David, Bill Masters, Bob Shaw.

[186] S08E12, "The Money," written by Peter Mehlman.

[187] S09E10, "The Strike," written by Dan O'Keefe, Alec Berg, Jeff Schaffer.

[188] S07E07, "The Secret Code," written by Alec Berg, Jeff Schaffer.

[189] S03E05, "The Library," written by Larry Charles.

[190] S03E22, "The Parking Space," written by Larry David, Greg Daniels.

[191] S05E16, "The Stand In," written by Larry David.

[192] S08E11, "The Little Jerry," written by Jennifer Crittenden.

[193] S09E13, "The Cartoon," written by Bruce Eric Kaplan.

[194] First in S04E08, "The Cheever Letters," written by Larry David, Elaine Pope, Tom Leopold.

[195] S06E24, "The Understudy," written by Marjorie Gross, Carol Leifer.

Comedian/B<expletive>d/Matey,[196] Mr. Steinfeld/Little Cable Boy,[197] Einstein,[198] Jugdish,[199] (The)[200] Sein,[201] The Good Son/Mr. Big Shot,[202] Dylan Murphy,[203] Big Baby/The Baby/Little Chicken Girl/The Nice Guy/Not a Man,[204] Buddy/Chunky/Tubby/Chubbs/Fatso/The Funny M<Expletive>er/Fat B<Expletive>d,[205] Mr. Goody Two Shoes,[206] Magnificent B<expletive>d,[207] Cowboy/Gerri,[208] Tragic Clown/Nucleus/Straw that Stirs the Drink/Miana,[209] Kind/Smart/Bad Man Very Very Bad Man,[210] Very Very Good/Lazy Man/Funny Guy,[211] The New Jerry,[212] Independent Jerry,[213] Mr. Nosy,[214] Black Saab/Kel Varnsen/Jackass,[215] Jerry Cougar Mellencamp/Back-up/Second-line/Just-in-case/B-plan of Contingency,[216] Tiger/Dough Boy/Daffodil/Butter Bean/Fat Guy,[217] Jerry Jerry Dingleberry/Seinsmelled,[218] Godfather/The Flincher,[219]

---

[196] S05E02, "The Puffy Shirt," written by Larry David.
[197] S02E10, "The Baby Shower," written by Larry Charles.
[198] S04E18, "The Old Man," written by Larry Charles.
[199] S09E08, "The Betrayal," written by David Mandel, Peter Mehlman.
[200] S04E23/24, "The Pilot," written by Larry David.
[201] First in S03E10, "The Stranded," written by Larry David, Jerry Seinfeld, Matt Goldman.
[202] S07E14/15, "The Cadillac," written by Larry David, Jerry Seinfeld.
[203] S03E19, "The Limo," written by Marc Jaffe, Larry Charles.
[204] S08E13, "The Comeback," written by Gregg Kavet, Andy Robin.
[205] S05E07, "The Non-Fat Yogurt," written by Larry David.
[206] S09E17, "The Bookstore," written by Spike Feresten, Darin Henry, Marc Jaffe.
[207] S08E20, "The Millennium," written by Jennifer Crittenden.
[208] S06E08, "The Mom & Pop Store," written by Tom Gammill, Max Pross.
[209] S04E09, "The Opera," written by Larry Charles.
[210] S03E07, "The Cafe," written by Tom Leopold.
[211] S04E15, "The Visa," written by Peter Mehlman.
[212] S09E03, "The Serenity Now," written by Steve Koren.
[213] S07E16, "The Shower Head," written by Peter Mehlman, Marjorie Gross.
[214] S09E01, "The Butter Shave," written by Alec Berg, Jeff Schaffer, David Mandel.
[215] S09E20, "The Puerto Rican Day," written by Alec Berg, Jennifer Crittenden, Spike Feresten, Bruce Eric Kaplan, Gregg Kavet, Steve Koren, David Mandel, Dan O'Keefe, Andy Robin, Jeff Schaffer.
[216] S01E01, "The Seinfeld Chronicles," written by Larry David, Jerry Seinfeld.
[217] S09E04, "The Blood," written by Dan O'Keefe.
[218] S04E20, "The Junior Mint," written by Andy Robin.
[219] S05E05, "The Bris," written by Larry Charles.

Jimmy,[220] Not Superman,[221] Jeromy,[222] Jer,[223] The Guy,[224] King of Comedy,[225] The Doofus,[226] Schmoopy,[227] Pal/Idiot Son,[228] #1 Dad/Seinfeld's Kid,[229] Sick Twisted Creep,[230] Sleepyhead,[231] Dandy/Fancy Boy,[232] Mr. Backstroke,[233] Gary,[234] Mr. Too Big to Come to My Shows/Crybaby,[235] JoJo/Funny Man/Seenfeld,[236] Archie,[237] Bizarro Kevin,[238] and The Lord of the Manor[239] - say? "What is the deal with testimonials? They're not testy, they're not monial. And what is the deal with statutes? Is it a statue where a 't' just snuck in? Is it statue or statute? You're positive it's statute?"[240] And accordingly you will say to them, as per the laws of the Festivus sacrifice, "We may not eat a dessert of choice after we are finished eating the Festivus sacrifice."

---

[220] First in S06E23, "The Face Painter," written by Larry David, Fred Stoller.

[221] S05E14, "The Marine Biologist," written by Ron Hauge, Charlie Rubin.

[222] S06E16, "The Beard," written by Carol Leifer.

[223] First in S04E14, "The Movie," written by Steve Skrovan, Bill Masters, Jon Hayman.

[224] S03E12, "The Red Dot," written by Larry David.

[225] S02E06, "The Statue," written by Larry Charles.

[226] S08E01, "The Foundation," written by Alec Berg, Jeff Schaffer.

[227] S07E06, "The Soup Nazi," written by Spike Feresten.

[228] S05E18/19, "The Raincoats," written by Tom Gammill, Max Pross, Larry David, Jerry Seinfeld.

[229] S08E17, "The English Patient," written by Steve Koren.

[230] S09E06, "The Merv Griffin Show," written by Bruce Eric Kaplan.

[231] S09E15, "The Wizard," written by Steve Lookner.

[232] S09E12, "The Reverse Peephole," written by Spike Feresten.

[233] S07E08, "The Pool Guy," written by David Mandel.

[234] S09E09, "The Apology," written by Jennifer Crittenden.

[235] S09E13, "The Cartoon," written by Bruce Eric Kaplan.

[236] S09E23/24, "The Finale," written by Larry David.

[237] S07E04, "The Wink," written by Tom Gammill, Max Pross.

[238] S08E03, "The Bizarro Jerry," written by David Mandel.

[239] S04E11, "The Contest," written by Larry David.

[240] S03E07, "The Cafe," written by Tom Leopold.

What does The Lord of the Idiots[241] person – also known as Art Vandelay,[242] Art Corvelay/Bert Harbinson,[243] Cantstandja,[244] Bootlegger,[245] Cartwright,[246] Baldy,[247] Humpty Dumpty with a Melon Head,[248] Body-Suit Man,[249] Georgie Boy,[250] The Urinator,[251] Cool Guy,[252] The Velvet Fog,[253] Colin/Donald O'Brien,[254] Georgie Porgie,[255] Caligula/The Fornicating Gourmet,[256] Architect,[257] Relationship/Independent/Movie/Coffee Shop/Liar/Bawdy/Gorgeous George,[258] Marine Biologist,[259] Mike,[260] Big Daddy,[261] Georgie C.,[262] Horrible Seed/Fine Seed/Bad Man/Good Boy/Bad Boy/Seed/Employee/Son/Friend/Fiancée/Dinner Guest/ Credit Risk/Date/Sport/Citizen/Tipper,[263] Koko the Monkey/Gammy/T-Bone/G-Bone,[264] Weak Spineless Man of Temptations/Sister/ Liar Man/J. Crew,[265]

---

[241] George appears in all episodes, but S03E03, "The Pen," written by Larry David.
[242] First used in S01E02, "The Stake Out," written by Larry David, Jerry Seinfeld, and many more times hence.
[243] Ibid. George's first alias attempts before settling on his go-to.
[244] S03E05, "The Library," written by Larry Charles.
[245] S08E04, "The Little Kicks," written by Spike Feresten.
[246] S02E11, "The Chinese Restaurant," written by Larry David, Jerry Seinfeld.
[247] S04E06, "The Watch," written by Larry David.
[248] S04E14, "The Movie," written by Steve Skrovan, Bill Masters, Jon Hayman.
[249] S08E20, "The Millennium," written by Jennifer Crittenden.
[250] S03E23, "The Keys," written by Larry Charles.
[251] S05E17, "The Wife," written by Peter Mehlman.
[252] S05E10, "The Cigar Store Indian," written by Tom Gammill, Max Pross.
[253] S06E19, "The Jimmy," written by Gregg Kavet, Andy Robin.
[254] S03E19, "The Limo," written by Marc Jaffe, Larry Charles.
[255] S03E12, "The Red Dot," written by Larry David.
[256] S09E04, "The Blood," written by Dan O'Keefe.
[257] First claimed in S01E02, "The Stake Out," written by Larry David, Jerry Seinfeld, and many more times after.
[258] S07E08, "The Pool Guy," written by David Mandel.
[259] S05E14, "The Marine Biologist," written by Ron Hauge, Charlie Rubin.
[260] S03E17/18, "The Boyfriend," written by Larry David, Larry Levin.
[261] S01E05, "The Stock Tip," written by Larry David, Jerry Seinfeld.
[262] S07E21/22, "The Bottle Deposit," written by Gregg Kavet, Andy Robin.
[263] S08E04, "The Little Kicks," written by Spike Feresten.
[264] S09E19, "The Maid," written by Alec Berg, David Mandel, Jeff Schaffer, Kit Boss, Peter Mehlman.
[265] S07E07, "The Secret Code," written by Alec Berg, Jeff Schaffer.

Chinless,[266] Slick,[267] Potsie,[268] Your Majesty/King Henry,[269] Perverted Little Weasel,[270] Eggplant/Mutant,[271] Stupid,[272] El Clowno,[273] Mr. Weatherbee,[274] Sleepy/Weasel,[275] Loman/Latex Salesman/Chucker,[276] Pear Shaped Loser,[277] Son of a <expletive>/Bastard,[278] The Opposite of Every Guy You've Ever Met,[279] King Edward VIII,[280] Importer Exporter,[281] Happy Camper/Sheriff,[282] Ollie,[283] Chorus Boy,[284] Joe Hollywood,[285] Brother Costanza,[286] Hand Model,[287] Come-With Guy,[288] Big Pop-in Guy,[289] Diana Ross,[290] Pappy,[291] Indiana,[292] Buck Naked,[293] Merlin,[294] Lover/Pretty Boy,[295] Bubble Boy/Puffball,[296] Little

---

[266] S08E10, "The Andrea Doria," written by Spike Feresten.

[267] S09E03, "The Serenity Now," written by Steve Koren.

[268] S06E20, "The Doodle," written by Alec Berg, Jeff Schaffer.

[269] S07E10, "The Gum," written by Tom Gammill, Max Pross.

[270] S05E04, "The Sniffing Accountant," written by Larry David, Jerry Seinfeld.

[271] S02E08, "The Heart Attack," written by Larry Charles.

[272] S07E03, "The Maestro," written by Larry David.

[273] S04E15, "The Visa," written by Peter Mehlman.

[274] S07E04, "The Wink," written by Tom Gammill, Max Pross.

[275] S09E04, "The Blood," written by Dan O'Keefe.

[276] S03E17/18, "The Boyfriend," written by Larry David, Larry Levin.

[277] S09E07, "The Slicer," written by Gregg Kavet, Andy Robin, Darin Henry.

[278] S07E05, "The Hot Tub," written by Gregg Kavet, Andy Robin.

[279] S05E22, "The Opposite," written by Andy Cowan, Larry David, Jerry Seinfeld.

[280] S05E11, "The Conversion," written by Bruce Kirschbaum.

[281] S07E14/15, "The Cadillac," written by Larry David, Jerry Seinfeld.

[282] S03E08, "The Tape," written by Larry David, Bob Shaw, Don McEnery.

[283] S06E01, "The Chaperone," written by Larry David, Bill Masters, Bob Shaw.

[284] S02E03, "The Jacket," written by Larry David, Jerry Seinfeld.

[285] S03E14, "The Pez Dispenser," written by Larry David.

[286] S05E11, "The Conversion," written by Bruce Kirschbaum.

[287] S05E02, "The Puffy Shirt," written by Larry David.

[288] S01E01, "The Seinfeld Chronicles," written by Larry David, Jerry Seinfeld.

[289] S03E21, "The Letter," written by Larry David.

[290] S04E01/02, "The Trip," written by Larry Charles

[291] S07E01, "The Engagement," written by Larry David.

[292] S03E22, "The Parking Space," written by Larry David, Greg Daniels.

[293] S04E17, "The Outing," written by Larry Charles.

[294] S08E08, "The Chicken Roaster," written by Alec Berg, Jeff Schaffer.

[295] S08E05, "The Package," written by Jennifer Crittenden.

[296] S05E13, "The Dinner Party," written by Larry David.

Sweetie Tweetie Weetie Weetie/Baby Bluey,[297] Mary,[298] Stupid Stupid Man,[299] Rhonda,[300] Le George,[301] The Bald Guy/Officer,[302] Mr. Gesundheit,[303] Aquaboy/Madam/Elton,[304] The Winter Me,[305] New Neil,[306] New Wilhelm/Hen Supervisor,[307] Closet Bania Fan,[308] Sweet Kid,[309] Buddy/Strange Man,[310] Kiddo,[311] Babydoll/Good Kid/Lovely Boy/Communist,[312] Little Man,[313] Animal,[314] Ginga/Dude,[315] Bald-again,[316] Bogambo,[317] That Guy,[318] Big Boy,[319] Monkey Boy,[320] Bizarro Gene,[321] and King of the County[322] - say? "Don't you think you get more without it?"[323] "To you" and not "to them." And since they exclude themselves from the community, they have denied a basic principle of agnosticism. And accordingly, you should blunt their

---

[297] S07E06, "The Soup Nazi," written by Spike Feresten.

[298] S03E01, "The Note," written by Larry David.

[299] S04E10, "The Virgin," written by Peter Mehlman, Peter Farrelly, Bobby Farrelly.

[300] S08E02, "The Soul Mate," written by Peter Mehlman.

[301] S09E11, "The Dealership," written by Steve Koren.

[302] S09E20, "The Puerto Rican Day," written by Alec Berg, Jennifer Crittenden, Spike Feresten, Bruce Eric Kaplan, Gregg Kavet, Steve Koren, David Mandel, Dan O'Keefe, Andy Robin, Jeff Schaffer.

[303] S03E20, "The Good Samaritan," written by Peter Mehlman.

[304] S05E03, "The Glasses," written by Tom Gammill, Max Pross.

[305] S09E05, "The Junk Mail," written by Spike Feresten.

[306] S08E17, "The English Patient," written by Steve Koren.

[307] S08E21, "The Muffin Tops," written by Spike Feresten.

[308] S09E01, "The Butter Shave," written by Alec Berg, Jeff Schaffer, David Mandel.

[309] S08E16, "The Pothole," written by Steve O'Donnell, Dan O'Keefe.

[310] S05E21, "The Hamptons," written by Peter Mehlman, Carol Leifer.

[311] S08E18, "The Nap," written by Gregg Kavet, Andy Robin.

[312] S09E23/24, "The Finale," written by Larry David.

[313] S06E07, "The Soup," written by Fred Stoller.

[314] S08E14, "The Van Buren Boys," written by Darin Henry.

[315] S05E12, "The Stall," written by Larry Charles.

[316] S06E16, "The Beard," written by Carol Leifer.

[317] S06E08, "The Mom & Pop Store," written by Tom Gammill, Max Pross.

[318] S09E17, "The Bookstore," written by Spike Feresten, Darin Henry, Marc Jaffe.

[319] S08E20, "The Millennium," written by Jennifer Crittenden.

[320] S06E11, "The Switch," written by Bruce Kirschbaum, Sam Kass.

[321] S08E03, "The Bizarro Jerry," written by David Mandel.

[322] S04E11, "The Contest," written by Larry David.

[323] S02E03, "The Jacket," written by Larry David, Jerry Seinfeld.

teeth by saying to them: "It is for the sake of this that Frank did for me when I shunned commercialism and religion. "For me" and not "for him." If he was there he would not have been redeemed."

What does The Hipster Doofus[324] person – also known as Jughead,[325] Vagabond,[326] Bagel Technician,[327] Krame,[328] Pops/Ball Man,[329] Class Champion,[330] Andre,[331] Coffee Boy,[332] Chuckles,[333] Assman,[334] H.E. Pennypacker: Industrialist/Philanthropist/Bicyclist,[335] Pimp Daddy,[336] Batman,[337] The Real J. Peterman,[338] Doc/Dr. Martin van Nostrand,[339] Numb Nuts,[340] Prof. Peter van Nostrand/Mr. von Nozzin,[341] The Smog Strangler,[342] Police Lineup Stand-in,[343] Kramerica Industries CEO,[344] Jerry's Friend/String Bean,[345] Man-child Crying Out for Love/Innocent Orphan in the Post-

[324] Kramer appears in all episodes, minus S02E11, "The Chinese Restaurant," written by Larry David, Jerry Seinfeld.
[325] S07E04, "The Wink," written by Tom Gammill, Max Pross.
[326] S08E14, "The Van Buren Boys," written by Darin Henry.
[327] S09E10, "The Strike," written by Dan O'Keefe, Alec Berg, Jeff Schaffer.
[328] S03E10, "The Stranded," written by Larry David, Jerry Seinfeld, Matt Goldman.
[329] S05E06, "The Lip Reader," written by Carol Leifer.
[330] S08E01, "The Foundation," written by Alec Berg, Jeff Schaffer.
[331] S05E12, "The Stall," written by Larry Charles.
[332] S07E02, "The Postponement," written by Larry David.
[333] S04E22, "The Handicap Spot," written by Larry David.
[334] S06E21, "The Fusilli Jerry," written by Marjorie Gross, Jonathan Gross, Ron Hauge, Charlie Rubin.
[335] S09E20, "The Puerto Rican Day," written by Alec Berg, Jennifer Crittenden, Spike Feresten, Bruce Eric Kaplan, Gregg Kavet, Steve Koren, David Mandel, Dan O'Keefe, Andy Robin, Jeff Schaffer.
[336] S07E19, "The Wig Master," written by Spike Feresten.
[337] S05E20, "The Fire," written by Larry Charles.
[338] S08E21, "The Muffin Tops," written by Spike Feresten.
[339] S09E07, "The Slicer," written by Gregg Kavet, Andy Robin, Darin Henry.
[340] S09E18, "The Frogger," written by Gregg Kavet, Andy Robin, Steve Koren, Dan O'Keefe.
[341] S03E09, "The Nose Job," written by Peter Mehlman.
[342] S04E01/02, "The Trip," written by Larry Charles
[343] S06E16, "The Beard," written by Carol Leifer.
[344] S09E02, "The Voice," written by Alec Berg, Jeff Schaffer, David Mandel.
[345] S09E13, "The Cartoon," written by Bruce Eric Kaplan.

modern World/Parasite/Sexually-depraved Miscreant Seeking to Gratify Only His Most Basic and Immediate Urges/Loathsome Offensive Brute/Huge Pop-in Guy,[346] Pod,[347] Ozzie Nelson,[348] Eddie,[349] Godfather,[350] K-Man,[351] Moviefone Man,[352] Mall Santa,[353] Stand In/Big Ape,[354] Hobo Joe,[355] Longshanks,[356] Bizarro Feldman,[357] Seat Filler,[358] El Presidente,[359] Bonkos,[360] Pinko/Commie/Traitor to Our Country,[361] Dad/Mr. President,[362] Steven Snell,[363] Bradley/Big Stupid Ape/Frankenstein,[364] Choochie,[365] Mack,[366] Not Kramer,[367] Kessler,[368] and Hoffman[369] - say? "Giddyup!"[370] You should say to them: "With a strong hand Frank took me out of commercialism and religion, from the houses of servitude."

---

[346] S03E21, "The Letter," written by Larry David.

[347] S02E05, "The Apartment," written by Peter Mehlman.

[348] S04E09, "The Opera," written by Larry Charles.

[349] S07E03, "The Maestro," written by Larry David.

[350] S05E05, "The Bris," written by Larry Charles.

[351] First in S05E08, "The Barber," written by Andy Robin.

[352] S07E08, "The Pool Guy," written by David Mandel.

[353] S06E10, "The Race," written by Tom Gammill, Max Pross, Larry David, Sam Kass.

[354] S05E16, "The Stand In," written by Larry David.

[355] S07E13, "The Seven," written by Alec Berg, Jeff Schaffer.

[356] S08E20, "The Millennium," written by Jennifer Crittenden.

[357] S08E03, "The Bizarro Jerry," written by David Mandel.

[358] S05E10, "The Summer of George," written by Alec Berg & Jeff Schaffer.

[359] S08E17, "The English Patient," written by Steve Koren.

[360] S05E22, "The Opposite," written by Andy Cowan, Larry David, Jerry Seinfeld.

[361] S06E10, "The Race," written by Tom Gammill, Max Pross, Larry David, Sam Kass.

[362] S09E15, "The Wizard," written by Steve Lookner.

[363] S03E23, "The Keys," written by Larry Charles.

[364] S07E23, "The Wait Out," written by Peter Mehlman, Matt Selman.

[365] S09E01, "The Butter Shave," written by Alec Berg, Jeff Schaffer, David Mandel.

[366] S08E07, "The Checks," written by Steve O'Donnell, Tom Gammill, Max Pross.

[367] S07E16, "The Shower Head," written by Peter Mehlman, Marjorie Gross.

[368] S01E01, "The Seinfeld Chronicles," written by Larry David, Jerry Seinfeld, and clarified in S09E08, "The Betrayal," written by David Mandel, Peter Mehlman.

[369] His name in the original script.

[370] First in S02E10, "The Baby Shower," written by Larry Charles, and muchly after.

And The Shiksappealing[371] person - also known as Nip,[372] Big Head,[373] Scab,[374] Gammy,[375] Carol,[376] La Madonna/Madre de Christo,[377] Deion,[378] Soul Sister,[379] Chesty La Rue,[380] Susie/Suze/Sharon/Dolt,[381] Lois,[382] Big Mouth,[383] The First Lady of the American Theater,[384] Nedda,[385] Nurse Paloma,[386] Sister,[387] Lois Loan,[388] Sally,[389] Not Lois Lane,[390] TR6,[391] Kid,[392] Beard,[393] Ned Isakoff,[394] Professor,[395] Baldist,[396] Lainey,[397] George,[398] President Lincoln/Scatterbrain,[399] The Janitor,[400] Wanda Pepper,[401] Calculating, Cold-hearted

[371] Elaine appears in all episodes, minus S01E01, "The Seinfeld Chronicles," written by Larry David, Jerry Seinfeld.
[372] S04E13, "The Pick," written by Larry David, Marc Jaffe.
[373] S08E10, "The Andrea Doria," written by Spike Feresten.
[374] S09E10, "The Strike," written by Dan O'Keefe, Alec Berg, Jeff Schaffer.
[375] S09E19, "The Maid," written by Alec Berg, David Mandel, Jeff Schaffer, Kit Boss, Peter Mehlman.
[376] S03E21, "The Letter," written by Larry David.
[377] S06E23, "The Face Painter," written by Larry David, Fred Stoller.
[378] S05E09, "The Masseuse," written by Peter Mehlman.
[379] S06E13, "The Scofflaw," written by Peter Mehlman.
[380] S07E10, "The Gum," written by Tom Gammill, Max Pross.
[381] S08E15, "The Susie," written by David Mandel.
[382] S06E08, "The Mom & Pop Store," written by Tom Gammill, Max Pross.
[383] S06E09, "The Secretary," written by Carol Leifer, Marjorie Gross.
[384] S05E01, "The Mango," written by Lawrence H. Levy, Larry David.
[385] S04E09, "The Opera," written by Larry Charles.
[386] S08E05, "The Package," written by Jennifer Crittenden.
[387] S07E16, "The Shower Head," written by Peter Mehlman, Marjorie Gross.
[388] S09E14, "The Strongbox," written by Dan O'Keefe, Billy Kimball.
[389] S08E04, "The Little Kicks," written by Spike Feresten.
[390] S05E14, "The Marine Biologist," written by Ron Hauge, Charlie Rubin.
[391] S05E15, "The Pie," written by Tom Gammill, Max Pross.
[392] S06E04, "The Chinese Woman," written by Peter Mehlman.
[393] S06E16, "The Beard," written by Carol Leifer.
[394] S06E10, "The Race," written by Tom Gammill, Max Pross, Larry David, Sam Kass.
[395] S03E07, "The Cafe," written by Tom Leopold.
[396] S03E08, "The Tape," written by Larry David, Bob Shaw, Don McEnery.
[397] First in S04E12, "The Airport," written by Larry Charles.
[398] S05E22, "The Opposite," written by Andy Cowan, Larry David, Jerry Seinfeld.
[399] S09E04, "The Blood," written by Dan O'Keefe.
[400] S08E16, "The Pothole," written by Steve O'Donnell, Dan O'Keefe.
[401] S03E09, "The Nose Job," written by Peter Mehlman.

Businesswoman/Sick Woman,[402] Miserable/The Office Tina Turner/Uncle Leo,[403] One Fine Looking Sexy Lady/The Woman,[404] Nancy Drew,[405] Super Lady,[406] Chick/Stupid,[407] Babe,[408] Ike,[409] Veronica,[410] and Queen of the Castle,[411] you start for them, as the non-sectarian scripture says: "And you should tell them on that day, saying 'It is for the sake of this that Frank did for me when I left commercialism and religion.'"

What do we say to The Cashier[412] person – also known as Ruthie Cohen? "Oh, hello, it's you! Listen lady, I got six minutes left on that meter, and I'm not budging till you admit you stole my twenty dollars. Huh-hu-hur, you're not so tough when you're not on your horse, are you Ruthie?" And she will say, "Your car's on fire. Merry Christmas."[413]

What does The Enigma, a Mystery Wrapped in a Riddle[414] person – also known as Chunky,[415] The White Whale/Scofflaw,[416] Big Daddy,[417] The Cleaner,[418] The Judge,[419] Newmie/Postman Agitator,[420] Tiny,[421]

[402] S08E13, "The Comeback," written by Gregg Kavet, Andy Robin.
[403] S09E17, "The Bookstore," written by Spike Feresten, Darin Henry, Marc Jaffe.
[404] S09E23/24, "The Finale," written by Larry David.
[405] S09E13, "The Cartoon," written by Bruce Eric Kaplan.
[406] S09E06, "The Merv Griffin Show," written by Bruce Eric Kaplan.
[407] S09E11, "The Dealership," written by Steve Koren.
[408] First in S05E12, "The Stall," written by Larry Charles.
[409] S06E01, "The Chaperone," written by Larry David, Bill Masters, Bob Shaw.
[410] S07E04, "The Wink," written by Tom Gammill, Max Pross.
[411] S04E11, "The Contest," written by Larry David.
[412] Ruthie appears in 101 episodes, a bit of trivia that surprise everyone. The actress Ruth Cohen passed in 2008. This is my nice little tribute. She deserves inclusion.
[413] S07E10, "The Gum," written by Tom Gammill, Max Pross.
[414] Newman appears in 46 episodes.
[415] S06E20, "The Doodle," written by Alec Berg, Jeff Schaffer.
[416] S06E13, "The Scofflaw," written by Peter Mehlman.
[417] S06E12, "The Label Maker," written by Alec Berg, Jeff Schaffer.
[418] S08E21, "The Muffin Tops," written by Spike Feresten.
[419] S07E13, "The Seven," written by Alec Berg, Jeff Schaffer.
[420] S09E12, "The Reverse Peephole," written by Spike Feresten.
[421] S03E23, "The Keys," written by Larry Charles.

Norman/The Fat Man/Magnificent B<expletive>d,[422] Pudgy,[423] That,[424] Postal Employee Newman,[425] Not Newman,[426] Certain Imbecile,[427] Simple Postal Worker,[428] Bizarro Vargas,[429] and Mystery Wrapped in a Twinkie[430] – say? "Where are they?" To this we should say, "In the back." He will be curt, and he will apologize, but as he will understand it, we have a situation here and time is of the essence.[431]

What does The Boss[432] person – also known as The Kaiser, King George, Head/Ruler of the Evil Empire, General Von Steingraber,[433] Manager George,[434] The Lion,[435] The Big Man,[436] The Bronx Bomber/Bomb Thrower, Yankee Doodle Dandy, Grandpa/Stein Pony Express,[437] Born on the Fourth of July, and Big Stein[438] – say? "I'm afraid I have some very sad news about your son." To him, we logically respond, "What the hell did you trade Jay Buhner for?"[439]

[422] S07E21/22, "The Bottle Deposit," written by Gregg Kavet, Andy Robin.
[423] S06E02, "The Big Salad," written by Larry David.
[424] S09E04, "The Blood," written by Dan O'Keefe.
[425] S09E05, "The Junk Mail," written by Spike Feresten.
[426] S07E16, "The Shower Head," written by Peter Mehlman, Marjorie Gross.
[427] S05E04, "The Sniffing Accountant," written by Larry David, Jerry Seinfeld.
[428] S09E23/24, "The Finale," written by Larry David.
[429] S08E03, "The Bizarro Jerry," written by David Mandel.
[430] S06E02, "The Big Salad," written by Larry David.
[431] S08E21, "The Muffin Tops," written by Spike Feresten.
[432] George Michael Steinbrenner III, 1930-2010, played by Lee Bear, voiced by Larry David, appears in 39 episodes. Actually 16, but David in 39. I need the comedic license to keep this section in its order, to maximize jokes and punchlines.
[433] RIP Bill Gallo, 1922-2011.
[434] Courtesy of Dallas Green.
[435] Sobriquet applied by Brian Cashman, Chief Building Rapeller, New York Yankees.
[436] S07E21/22, "The Bottle Deposit," written by Gregg Kavet, Andy Robin.
[437] S08E18, "The Nap," written by Gregg Kavet, Andy Robin.
[438] S07E20, "The Calzone," written by Alec Berg, Jeff Schaffer.
[439] S07E12, "The Caddy," written by Gregg Kavet, Andy Robin.

What does The Belligerent Patriarch[440] person – also known as Chef,[441] Salesman,[442] Casanova,[443] and Your Father[444] – say? "George, Festivus is your heritage – it's part of who you are." To which we say, "Oh, God."

What does The Put-upon Team-Switching Fiancee [445] person – also known as Lily[446] – say? "I just want you to know that I love your son very much." To which the Melodramatic Matriarch says, "May I ask why?"[447]

What does The Melodramatic Matriarch[448] person – also known as Your Mother[449] and Jimmy Arms[450] – say? "I go out for a quart of milk, I come home, and find my son treating his body like it was an amusement park!" To which the Lord of the Idiots says, "Ma, people can hear you."[451]

What does The Number-crunching Yiddishe Tatte[452] person – also known as Mr. President,[453] Raincoat Salesman,[454] and Intern at Best[455] – say? "Do you know what the interest on that fifty dollars comes to over fifty-three years? Six hundred and sixty-three dollars and forty-five cents. And that's figuring conservatively

[440] Frank Costanza appears in 29 episodes.
[441] S08E06, "The Fatigues," written by Gregg Kavet, Andy Robin.
[442] Christian relics: S06E24, "The Understudy," written by Marjorie Gross, Carol Leifer; manssiere: S06E18, "The Doorman," written by Tom Gammill, Max Pross.
[443] S05E18/19, "The Raincoats," written by Tom Gammill, Max Pross, Larry David, Jerry Seinfeld.
[444] Ad nauseam, mostly by the Melodramatic Matriarch.
[445] Susan Ross appears in 29 episodes.
[446] S07E24, "The Invitations," written by Larry David.
[447] S07E01, "The Engagement," written by Larry David.
[448] Estelle Costanza appears in 27 episodes.
[449] Ad nauseam, mostly by the Belligerent Patriarch and The Comedian.
[450] S08E12, "The Money," written by Peter Mehlman.
[451] S04E11, "The Contest," written by Larry David.
[452] Morty Seinfeld appears in 24 episodes.
[453] Of the tenant's board of The Pines of Mar Gables, Phase II.
[454] S05E18/19, "The Raincoats," written by Tom Gammill, Max Pross, Larry David, Jerry Seinfeld.
[455] S08E12, "The Money," written by Peter Mehlman.

at five percent interest, over fifty-three years, compounded quarterly. Or, if you put it into a ten-year T-bill..." To which the Ever-doting Yiddishe Mamme says, "Morty, will you stop it?"[456]

What does The Ever-doting Yiddishe Mamme[457] person – also known as First Lady – say, about The Comedian? "How can anyone not like you? You're a wonderful, wonderful boy. Everybody likes you. It's impossible not to like you. Impossible. Morty?" To which the Number-crunching Yiddishe Tatte says, "Maybe some people don't like him. I could see that."[458]

What does The Noir-Voiced World-traveling Adventurer[459] person – also known as Mr. Peterson[460] - say? "I like that shirt. Where did you get it?" To which The Shiksappealing says, "Oh, this innocent looking shirt has something which isn't innocent at all. Touchability! Heavy, silky Italian cotton, with a fine almost terrycloth like feeling. Five button placket, relaxed fit, innocence and mayhem at once."

That's not bad.[461]

What does The Old Coot[462] person – also known as Book Thief[463] – say? "Why didn't ya say hello?" To which The Comedian says, "Because you were too busy stealing a book."[464]

---

[456] S06E17, "The Kiss Hello," written by Larry David, Jerry Seinfeld.
[457] Helen Seinfeld appears in 24 episodes.
[458] S04E05, "The Wallet," written by Larry David.
[459] Jacopo "J." Peterman appears in 22 episodes.
[460] S08E14, "The Van Buren Boys," written by Darin Henry.
[461] S06E24, "The Understudy," written by Marjorie Gross, Carol Leifer.
[462] Uncle Leo appears in 15 episodes.
[463] S09E17, "The Bookstore," written by Spike Feresten, Darin Henry, Marc Jaffe.
[464] Ibid.

What does The Forgetful Supervisor[465] person – also known as Tania[466] - say? "Is there something wrong?" To which The Lord of the Idiots says...nothing. He winks. The Forgetful Supervisor will understand.[467]

What does The Mimboyfriend[468] person – also known as Face Painter/El Diablo,[469] Grease Monkey,[470] and Car Salesman[471] – say? "Yeah, that's right." To which we say...nothing, because that's kind of a conversation ender.

But he'll be back; we'll make out.[472]

---

[465] Matt Wilhelm appears in 12 episodes.

[466] S08E07, "The Checks," written by Steve O'Donnell, Tom Gammill, Max Pross.

[467] S07E04, "The Wink," written by Tom Gammill, Max Pross.

[468] David Puddy appears in 11 episodes.

[469] S06E23, "The Face Painter," written by Larry David, Fred Stoller.

[470] S06E21, "The Fusilli Jerry," written by Marjorie Gross, Jonathan Gross, Ron Hauge, Charlie Rubin.

[471] S09E11, "The Dealership," written by Steve Koren.

[472] S06E23, "The Face Painter," written by Larry David, Fred Stoller.

From the Beginning of the Month

All Right, Okay. Let's Go, Details.[473]

It could be from the beginning of the month that one would have to discuss the Festivus. However, we learn otherwise, since it is stated, "on that day." If it is written "on that day," it could be from while it is still day before the night of the twenty-third day of the twelfth month. However we learn otherwise, since it is stated, "for the sake of this." I did not say "for the sake of this" except that it be observed when this meatloaf and bitter greens are resting in front of you, meaning, on the night of the twenty-third.

For if you have too much time, then you could have a month and a half to come up with something and not do anything.[474]

But if you expound on the Festivus story to your delight on the appropriate time, then you could spend a month there one night.[475]

Bottom line: it is not a night to be speechless, to have no speech, to be without speech.[476]

---

[473] S02E09, "The Deal," written by Larry David.
[474] S04E10, "The Virgin," written by Peter Mehlman, Peter Farrelly, Bobby Farrelly.
[475] S09E06, "The Merv Griffin Show," written by Bruce Eric Kaplan.
[476] S03E20, "The Good Samaritan," written by Peter Mehlman.

In the Beginning Our Fathers Were God Worshipers

We Hate the Big Brokerage Houses. Hate Them with a Passion.[477]

Yada yada yada,[478] [479] Frank is great.

He covers the marble ryes[480] and lifts up the cup of Ovaltine – or Postum, which should be a more popular drink[481] - and says:

> And it is this that has stood for our ancestors and for us; since it is not only one company or religious order that has stood against us to destroy us, but rather in each generation, they stand against us to destroy us, but the Frank One, blessed be He, rescues us from their hand.

---

[477] S03E13, "The Subway," written by Larry Charles.

[478] S08E19, "The Yada Yada," written by Peter Mehlman, Jill Franklin.

[479] What is this use of "Yada Yada" exactly? Well, you do realize that I'm squeezing blood from a stone here. Festivus takes up 4:38 of air time in an episode not even named after the holiday. This is the first section where I simply couldn't figure out how to translate or fuse the material into the Seinfeld canon, what with references to biblical characters with no analog to series characters, crossing rivers, and other epic events for which I couldn't find a good metaphor. Therefore, I reserve the right to invoke this four times, at most, so the material can stay sharp, focused, and undiluted.

[480] Marbles rye?

[481] S03E14, "The Pez Dispenser," written by Larry David.

First Fruits Declaration

What the Hell Does That Mean?[482] [483]

The head of household puts down the cup of Ovaltine - or if he likes, loves, is crazy about, or lives for Merlot, then he can have Merlot, unless he's out of Merlot[484] - from his hand and uncovers the marbles rye.[485]

Yada yada yada,[486] Frank is great.

---

[482] S08E04, "The Little Kicks," written by Spike Feresten.

[483] It means whatever the hell you want it to mean.

[484] S08E19, "The Yada Yada," written by Peter Mehlman, Jill Franklin.

[485] Marble ryes?

[486] That's two, because man, if it was difficult to fuse material from this section to the Seinfeld universe with my first yada yada, then this doubles-down big time. Two left.

The Twenty Plagues

Aside from Meningitis, Scoliosis, or Lupus, Is It Lupus?[487]

When the head of household says, "Blood and fire and pillars of smoke" and the twenty plagues and the "PSBAAC'S," "TSDBR'R," and "DDDTAB'U" mnemonic, all present should pour out a little Ovaltine, or Bosco,[488] from their cup, or use a spoon or their pinky finger to sprinkle onto a napkin or plate.

Blood and fire and pillars of smoke.

Another explanation for the verse "And the Frank took us out of Bayside with feats of strength[489] and with an outstretched rocket for a forearm[490] and with great shell-shock[491] and awe and with signs of protest[492] and with amazing, albeit somewhat inappropriate, wonders" [493] (Costanzonomy 26:8) is as follows: "With feats of strength" corresponds to four plagues; "and with an outstretched rocket for a forearm" corresponds to four plagues; "and with great shell-shock and awe" corresponds to four plagues; "and with signs of protest" corresponds to four plagues; "and with amazing, albeit somewhat inappropriate, wonders" corresponds to four plagues.

---

[487] A frequent freakout of George's, first fretted over in S02E08, "The Heart Attack," written by Larry Charles, and twice more in S03E15, "The Suicide," written by Tom Leopold.

[488] S07E07, "The Secret Code," written by Alec Berg, Jeff Schaffer.

[489] You should know which episode this references by now.

[490] S07E12, "The Caddy," written by Gregg Kavet, Andy Robin.

[491] S08E06, "The Fatigues," written by Gregg Kavet, Andy Robin

[492] Such as the aforementioned "Festivus Yes, Bagels No."

[493] Such as "Let me understand. You got the hen, the chicken and the rooster. The rooster goes with the chicken. So, who's having sex with the hen?" from S07E11, "The Rye," written by Carol Leifer.

These are the twenty plagues - I mean the plague! Please![494] - that the Frank One, blessed be He, brought on the corporations and religions in Bayside, and they are:

Protests

Strikes

Boycotts

Audits

Activism

Competition

Social Media Shaming

Trust Busting

Socialism

Divestiture

Bitcoin

Re-education

Renunciation

Disaffiliation

Disengagement

Defection

Tergiversation

Apostasy

Bill Maher

Uromysitis Poisoning[495]

---

[494] S09E08, "The Betrayal," written by David Mandel, Peter Mehlman.
[495] S03E06, "The Parking Garage," written by Larry David.

Enough for Us

Or, I Got a Real Problem With You People[496]

How many degrees of good did Frank bestow upon us!

If He had gone shopping for a doll for his son, and there would have been more than one left; it would have been enough for us.

If there was only one doll left, and another shopper did not also want the same one; it would have been enough for us.

If the other shopper wanted the same one, and Frank did not rain blows upon him; it would have been enough for us.

If Frank rained blows upon him, but would not have realized there must be another way; it would have been enough for us.

If He realized there must be another way, and not created Festivus as a result; it would have been enough for us.

If He created Festivus, but had not created the Airing of Grievances; it would have been enough for us.

If He had created the Airing of Grievances, but had not instituted the pole; it would have been enough for us.

If He had instituted the pole, but had not found tinsel distracting; it would have been enough for us.

If He found tinsel distracting, but had not introduced the Feats of Strength; it would have been enough for us.

---

[496] And now you're gonna hear about it!

If He had introduced the Feats of Strength, but had not included the telling of Festivus Miracles; it would have been enough for us.

If He had included the telling of Festivus Miracles, but had failed to record previous Festivuses;[497] it would have been enough for us.

If He had recorded previous Festivi,[498] but Kramer had not revived the holiday; it would have been enough for us.

Had Kramer revived the holiday, but George had not established The Human Fund; it would have been enough for us.

How much more so is the good that is doubled and quadrupled that Frank bestowed upon us enough for us; since He went shopping for the doll, and it was the last one; and fought a stranger for it; and realized there must be a better way; and created Festivus; and fashioned the Airing of Grievances; and declared an aluminum pole; and found tinsel distracting; and willed the Feats of Strength into being; and commanded the telling of Festivus Miracles; and recorded the previous Festivus dinners; and told over the mysteries to Kramer; and The Human Fund was incorporated.

---

[497] Festivi?
[498] Festivuses?

Rabbi Cosmo's Three Things

We have to do it. It's part of our lifestyle.[499]

Rabbi Cosmo was accustomed to say, "Anyone who has not done these three things on Festivus has not fulfilled his obligation, and these are them: the Festivus Pole, meatloaf, and Airing of Grievances."

He holds the pole in his hand and shows it to the others there.

The Festivus Pole that our ancestors were accustomed to using when Queens Boulevard existed, for the sake of what was it? For the sake to commemorate that the Frank One, blessed be He, passed through the homes of our ancestors in Bayside, as it is stated (Kramerus 12:27); "And you shall say: 'It is the Festivus Pole to the Frank One, for that He passed through the homes of the Children of Queens Boulevard in Bayside, when He smote the corporations and religions, and our homes he saved.' And the people bowed the head and bowed."

He holds the meatloaf in his hand and shows it to the others there.

This meatloaf that we are eating, for the sake of what is it? For the sake to commemorate that our ancestors' meat patties were not yet able to rise, before the King of the kings of Queens, the Frank One, blessed be He, revealed Himself to them and redeemed them, as it is stated (Kramerus 12:39); "And they cooked the meats which they brought out of Bayside into meat loaves, since it did not rise; because they were expelled from Bayside, and could not tarry, neither had they made for themselves provisions."

---

[499] S04E11, "The Contest," written by Larry David.

He holds the bitters in his hand and shows it to the others there.

> These bitter greens that we are eating and grievances that we are airing, for the sake of what are they? For the sake to commemorate that the corporations and religions embittered the lives of our ancestors in Bayside, as it is stated (Kramerus 1:14); "And they made their lives bitter with price gouging, in cost and in interest rates, and in all manner of service to gods; in all their service to these entities, wherein they made them serve with rigor."

> In each and every generation, a person is obligated to see himself as if he left Bayside, as it is stated (Kramerus 13:8); "For the sake of this, did Frank do this for me in my going out of Bayside." Not only our ancestors did the Frank One, blessed be He, redeem, but rather also us together with them did He redeem, as it is stated (Costanzonomy 6:23); "And He took us out from there, in order to bring us in, to give us the retirement community which He swore unto our fathers."

> Particularly, one Morty Seinfeld.

> Who swore in return that he could not return to Florida.[500]

---

[500] S07E16, "The Shower Head," written by Peter Mehlman, Marjorie Gross.

First Half of Praise

Said with an Unblemished Record of Staunch Heterosexuality[501]

The head of household holds the cup of Ovaltine – or Yoohoo, a fine product[502] - in his hand, and he covers the ryes marble[503] and says:

> Therefore we are obligated to thank, praise, laud, glorify, exalt, lavish, bless, raise high, and acclaim He who made all these miracles for our ancestors and for us: He brought us out from slavery to freedom, from sorrow to joy, from mourning to celebration of a festival, from darkness to great light, and from servitude to redemption. And let us say a new song before Him, Halleluyah!

> Halleluyah! Praise, servants of the Frank, praise the name of the Frank. May the Name of the Frank be blessed from now and forever. From the rising of the sun in the East to its setting, the name of the Frank is praised. Above all nations is-

In some communities, the reading is kiboshed[504] here, and all instead say:

> Yada yada yada,[505] Frank is great.

Because this is laying it on a bit thick, don't you think?[506]

Was that wrong? Should we not have done that?[507]

---

[501] S02E03, "The Jacket," written by Larry David, Jerry Seinfeld.
[502] S04E07, "The Bubble Boy," written by Larry David, Larry Charles.
[503] That should end the confusion.
[504] S04E09, "The Opera," written by Larry Charles.
[505] That's three. One to go.
[506] S05E01, "The Mango," written by Lawrence H. Levy, Larry David.
[507] S03E12, "The Red Dot," written by Larry David.

Second Cup of Ovaltine

You Know About the Uh, Cup Sizes and All?[508]

We raise the cup of Ovaltine – or schnapps, which can get you pretty loaded[509] - until we reach "who redeemed the subjugated people."

> Blessed are You, Frank our Founder, Master of His Household, who redeemed us and redeemed our ancestors from overlords of commercialism and religion, and brought us on this night to eat meatloaf and marble rye; so too, Frank our Founder, and Founder of our Festivus adherents, bring us to other appointed times and holidays[510] that will come to greet us in peace, joyful in the building of Your retirement home and happy in Your worship; that we shall eat there from the offerings and from the Festivus sacrifices, the blood of which shall reach the wall of Your altar for favor, and we shall thank You with a new song upon our redemption and upon the restoration of our souls. Blessed are you, Frank, who redeemed the subjugated people.

We say the blessing below and drink the cup while making a move to the left. Can't go right.[511]

> Blessed are You, Frank our Founder, who creates the Festivus holiday.

---

[508] S05E04, "The Sniffing Accountant," written by Larry David, Jerry Seinfeld.

[509] S09E08, "The Betrayal," written by David Mandel, Peter Mehlman.

[510] A Holidus for all of us?

[511] S04E19, "The Implant," written by Peter Mehlman.

Washing

Maybe Downgrade to the Cyclone F Series or Hyrda Jet Flow[512]

We wash the hands and make the blessing.

> Blessed are You, Frank our Founder, Master of His Household, who has desanctified us with His commandments and has commanded us on the washing of the hands.

If you do not, it is like telling him you want a piece of him, and could drop him like a bag of dirt.

And if you want a piece of him, you got it.[513]

---

[512] S07E16, "The Shower Head," written by Peter Mehlman, Marjorie Gross.
[513] S08E04, "The Little Kicks," written by Spike Feresten.

Who Puts Out the Marble Rye

If You Forget, It's Deliberate! Deliberate, I Tell Ya![514]

The head of household takes out the marble ryes in the order that he placed them, the broken one between the two whole ones; he holds the three of them in his hand and blesses "who brings forth" with the intention to take from the top one and "on eating marble" with the intention of eating from the broken one. Afterwards, he breaks off a Mackinaw peach's measure from the top whole one and a second Mackinaw peach's measure from the broken one and he dips them into paella and eats both while reclining.

> Blessed are You, Frank our Founder, Master of His Household, who brings forth marble rye from Schnitzer's.

> Blessed are You, Frank our Founder, Master of His Household, who has desanctified us with His commandments and has commanded us on the eating of marble rye.

> And kasha.[515]

---

[514] S07E11, "The Rye," written by Carol Leifer.
[515] S06E18, "The Doorman," written by Tom Gammill, Max Pross.

Bitter Herbs

You Don't Try and Sour. You Have to De-sweeten Too![516]

All present should take a Mackinaw peach's measure of bitter herbs, dip into the paella,[517] shake off the extra paella,[518] make the blessing, and eat without reclining.

> Blessed are You, Frank our Founder, Master of His Household, who has desanctified us with His commandments and has commanded us on the eating of bitter herbs.

This is, of course, metaphor, but you must now commence with the literal Airing of Grievances. The head of household shall begin by making general statements against all present, then letting the professional superior of one's offspring have it, followed by humiliating said offspring, then working counterclockwise around the table before handing off to the first person on the right. Each person who speaks may only do so while grasping the pole.[519]

---

[516] S07E18, "The Friar's Club," written by David Mandel.
[517] S05E18/19, "The Raincoats," written by Tom Gammill, Max Pross, Larry David, Jerry Seinfeld.
[518] Ibid.
[519] Bylaw unearthed via "Festivus, the Holiday for the Rest of Us," by Allen Salkin.

Sandwich

Because So Much Depends On the Layering[520]

All present should take a Mackinaw peach's measure from the third whole meatloaf with a Mackinaw peach's measure of mustard,[521] wrap them together and eat them while reclining and without saying a blessing. Before one eats it, one should say:

> In memory of Queensboro Plaza according to Kramer. This is what Kramer would do when the gyro stand[522] existed:

> He would tie his shoelaces, get his three dollars ready, gun for the stand where the gyros with meatloaf and mustard were cooked, and wrapped, and ready to go, and eat them together, in order to fulfill what is stated, (Kramerus 12:15): "You should eat it upon meatloaf and mustards."

[520] S01E01, "The Seinfeld Chronicles," written by Larry David, Jerry Seinfeld.
[521] S07E13, "The Seven," written by Alec Berg, Jeff Schaffer.
[522] S05E10, "The Cigar Store Indian," written by Tom Gammill, Max Pross.

The Dinner Part-y[523]

No Saving the Meal for Another Time[524]

We eat and drink.

Avoid pony remarks,[525] elbow grabbing,[526] rescuing partly-eaten dessert from the receptacle,[527] fishing for rye bread,[528] discussing which barn fowl goes with which,[529] excessive beefarino,[530] advising a store owner to change his motif,[531] swallowing flies,[532] trusting the gamble that is cantaloupe,[533] hiding mutton,[534] recommending nose jobs,[535] double-dipping,[536] trifectas,[537] lip reading,[538] low-talking,[539] squirting grapefruit juice in people's eyes,[540] putting your face in someone's soup and blowing,[541] visualizing your neighbor as a roasted turkey,[542] sitting on pasta statues,[543] tendering "God bless you"s to persons before allowing their spouses reasonable time to administer their own,[544] eating peanut butter out of a jar with your disgusting

---

[523] S05E13, "The Dinner Party," written by Larry David.
[524] S06E07, "The Soup," written by Fred Stoller.
[525] S02E02, "The Pony Remark," written by Larry David, Jerry Seinfeld.
[526] Ibid.
[527] S06E06, "The Gymnast," written by Alec Berg, Jeff Schaffer.
[528] S07E11, "The Rye," written by Carol Leifer.
[529] Ibid.
[530] Ibid.
[531] S03E07, "The Café," written by Tom Leopold.
[532] S02E01, "The Ex-Girlfriend," written by Larry David, Jerry Seinfeld.
[533] Ibid.
[534] S07E04, "The Wink," written by Tom Gammill, Max Pross.
[535] S03E09, "The Nose Job," written by Peter Mehlman.
[536] S04E19, "The Implant," written by Peter Mehlman.
[537] S09E04, "The Blood," written by Dan O'Keefe.
[538] S05E06, "The Lip Reader," written by Carol Leifer.
[539] S05E02, "The Puffy Shirt," written by Larry David.
[540] Ibid.
[541] S02E11, "The Chinese Restaurant," written by Larry David, Jerry Seinfeld.
[542] S09E01, "The Butter Shave," written by Alec Berg, Jeff Schaffer, David Mandel.
[543] S06E21, "The Fusilli Jerry," written by Marjorie Gross, Jonathan Gross, Ron Hauge, Charlie Rubin.
[544] S03E20, "The Good Samaritan," written by Peter Mehlman.

index fingers,[545] having poppy seed muffins before drug testing,[546] leaving a glass near the edge of the table,[547] scarfing 60-year-old wedding cake,[548] positing that dingoes ate one's baby,[549] downing hot dogs from the Silent Era,[550] obsessing over calzones,[551] having your shirt overcooked,[552] turning down Junior Mints,[553] dining on poached lobster,[554] masticating pre-masticated pecans,[555] having just salad if you're a man,[556] slipping anyone a mickey,[557] inspecting your mother's bra,[558] taking books to the bathroom,[559] mistaking onions for apples,[560] frequenting places where the chefs are sloppy,[561] unbonding with males,[562] using utensils for candy bars,[563] blaming busboys for starting fires,[564] trusting non-fat yogurt,[565] scratching your face with your middle finger,[566] doing full bodied dry heaves set to music,[567] drinking spoiled milk,[568] tucking into hair with cake around it, [569] munching pretzels that make you thirsty,[570] inhaling ice cream,[571]

[545] S04E05, "The Wallet," written by Larry David.

[546] S07E16, "The Shower Head," written by Peter Mehlman, Marjorie Gross.

[547] S05E05, "The Bris," written by Larry Charles.

[548] S09E18, "The Frogger," written by Gregg Kavet, Andy Robin, Steve Koren, Dan O'Keefe.

[549] S03E10, "The Stranded," written by Larry David, Jerry Seinfeld, Matt Goldman.

[550] S07E10, "The Gum," written by Tom Gammill, Max Pross.

[551] S07E20, "The Calzone," written by Alec Berg, Jeff Schaffer.

[552] Ibid.

[553] S04E20, "The Junior Mint," written by Andy Robin.

[554] S05E21, "The Hamptons," written by Peter Mehlman, Carol Leifer.

[555] S06E20, "The Doodle," written by Alec Berg, Jeff Schaffer.

[556] S07E04, "The Wink," written by Tom Gammill, Max Pross.

[557] S02E07, "The Revenge," written by Larry David.

[558] S05E04, "The Sniffing Accountant," written by Larry David, Jerry Seinfeld.

[559] S09E17, "The Bookstore," written by Spike Feresten, Darin Henry, Marc Jaffe.

[560] S05E03, "The Glasses," written by Tom Gammill, Max Pross.

[561] S05E15, "The Pie," written by Tom Gammill, Max Pross.

[562] S01E04, "Male Unbonding," written by Larry David, Jerry Seinfeld.

[563] S06E03, "The Pledge Drive," written by Tom Gammill, Max Pross.

[564] S02E12, "The Busboy," written by Larry David, Jerry Seinfeld.

[565] S05E07, "The Non-Fat Yogurt," written by Larry David.

[566] S06E03, "The Pledge Drive," written by Tom Gammill, Max Pross.

[567] S08E04, "The Little Kicks," written by Spike Feresten.

[568] S04E01/02, "The Trip," written by Larry Charles

[569] S05E13, "The Dinner Party," written by Larry David.

[570] S03E11, "The Alternate Side," written by Larry David, Bill Masters.

[571] S05E06, "The Lip Reader," written by Carol Leifer.

consuming shower salads,[572] buying supermarket fruit,[573] Pez,[574] black and white cookies,[575] and popping shirtless out of the bathroom.[576]

[572] S09E09, "The Apology," written by Jennifer Crittenden.
[573] S05E01, "The Mango," written by Lawrence H. Levy, Larry David.
[574] S03E14, "The Pez Dispenser," written by Larry David.
[575] Ibid.
[576] S06E06, "The Gymnast," written by Alec Berg, Jeff Schaffer.

The Hidden (Big Salad)

Check Under the Ofice Desk, People Hide There[577]

After the end of the meal – following a week-long game of hide-and-seek[578] and blackmail with the children - all those present take a Mackinaw peach's measure from the Big Salad, that was concealed for the afikovorkah, and eat it from it while reclining.

Before eating the afikavorkah, all should say: "In memory of the Festivus sacrifice that was eaten upon being satiated."

We do not serve cake after the meal. It would indeed kill the hosts to put out some pound cake or something. Traditionally, this is neither impolite, nor stupid.

Covfefe[579] may be served.[580]

Now, if you have made it this far and are still together with your boyfriend, take stock of your relationship while negotiations ensue, and consider dumping him if you believe the shrinkage rumors to be true.[581]

Or if another woman's hate for him trumps your like for him.[582]

Or if he convinced you to get a ruinous nose job.[583]

Or if he had hand, and is gonna need it.[584]

Or if he cheated on his IQ test.[585]

---

[577] S03E12, "The Red Dot," written by Larry David.
[578] S03E21, "The Letter," written by Larry David.
[579] Autocorrect didn't correct that! Whoa!
[580] S07E11, "The Rye," written by Carol Leifer.
[581] S05E21, "The Hamptons," written by Peter Mehlman, Carol Leifer.
[582] S05E09, "The Masseuse," written by Peter Mehlman.
[583] S03E09, "The Nose Job," written by Peter Mehlman.
[584] S03E14, "The Pez Dispenser," written by Larry David.
[585] S03E07, "The Cafe," written by Tom Leopold.

Or if you are not as dark and disturbed (and depressed and inadequate) as your best friend.[586]

Or if you found him, so you can break up with him.[587]

Or if he gave you a cashmere sweater just to shut you up, but it had a red dot on it.[588]

Or if you will be doing six to eight months for shoplifting.[589]

Or if he obsessively demands a thank you for the Big Salad.[590]

Or if he stalks you to bathrooms because he thinks you're refunding.[591]

Or if you are going back to Latvia for a year.[592]

Or if he is not bald enough, especially in comparison to you.[593]

Or because you do not love him, even if you heard him the first time.[594]

Or if he wrote The Move directions on his hand, despite that you enjoyed the results.[595]

Or if it is not him, it is you – even though he invented the "It's not you, it's me" routine.[596]

Or if he trampled women and children because he thought there was a fire.[597]

Or if you did not find his dissertation on manure to be particularly thrilling.[598]

---

[586] S04E15, "The Visa," written by Peter Mehlman.
[587] S08E15, "The Susie," written by David Mandel.
[588] S03E12, "The Red Dot," written by Larry David.
[589] S08E19, "The Yada Yada," written by Peter Mehlman, Jill Franklin.
[590] S06E02, "The Big Salad," written by Larry David.
[591] S06E11, "The Switch," written by Bruce Kirschbaum, Sam Kass.
[592] S05E11, "The Conversion," written by Bruce Kirschbaum.
[593] S06E16, "The Beard," written by Carol Leifer.
[594] S06E23, "The Face Painter," written by Larry David, Fred Stoller.
[595] S06E21, "The Fusilli Jerry," written by Marjorie Gross, Jonathan Gross, Ron Hauge, Charlie Rubin.
[596] S05E06, "The Lip Reader," written by Carol Leifer.
[597] S05E20, "The Fire," written by Larry Charles.
[598] S06E07, "The Soup," written by Fred Stoller.

Or just punch him in the face because he's engaged.[599]

---

[599] S07E14/15, "The Cadillac," written by Larry David, Jerry Seinfeld.

Bless

Or, You're soo Good Lookin'[600]

---

[600] S03E20, "The Good Samaritan," written by Peter Mehlman.

Grace After Meals

That's It! We've Had Enough![601]

We pour the third cup of Ovaltine – or prune juice, if it's the only thing you have that's chilled[602] - and recite the Grace over the food.

Not many people have grace. Grace is a tough one. You can't have a little grace. You either have grace, or you don't, and you can't acquire grace or pick it up at the market.

With that positive introduction, let us say grace – even if you don't have grace or don't want grace. [603]

> A Song of Ascents; When the Frank will bring back the captivity of Del Boca Vista, we will be like dreamers. Then our mouth will be full of mirth and our tongue joyful melody; then they will say among the corporations and sects; "The Frank has done greatly with these." The Frank has done great things for us; we are happy. Frank, return our captivity like streams in the desert. Those that sow with tears will reap with joyful song. He who surely goes and cries, he carries the measure of seed, he will surely come in joyful song and carry his sheaves. (Balms[604] 126)

Three that ate together are obligated to introduce the blessing and the leader of the introduction opens as follows:

> Okay.

All those present answer:

> Let's go.

---

[601] S02E02, "The Pony Remark," written by Larry David, Jerry Seinfeld.
[602] S05E10, "The Cigar Store Indian," written by Tom Gammill, Max Pross.
[603] S06E01, "The Chaperone," written by Larry David, Bill Masters, Bob Shaw.
[604] S07E03, "The Maestro," written by Larry David.

The leader says:

Here we are.

Those present answer:

Right now.

The leader says:

Let's do it.

Those present answer:

You and me.

The leader says:

Okay.

Those present answer:

Alright.

The leader says:

What'dya got?[605]

They all say:

Blessed are You, Frank our Founder, Head of His Household, who nourishes all in His goodness,[606] in grace, kindness, and mercy;[607] He gives marble rye to all flesh since His kindness is forever.[608] And in His goodness, we have not lacked, and may we not lack nourishment ever and always, for His great name. For He is a Power that feeds and provides all and does good to all and prepares nourishment for all creatures that he created.[609] Blessed are You, Frank, who sustains all.

---

[605] S04E08, "The Cheever Letters," written by Larry David, Elaine Pope, Tom Leopold.

[606] Well, certainly, at least, the U.S. Army, and the Jewish singles.

[607] Okay, fine, stretching it a bit.

[608] But if his hosts don't serve it, he can take it back.

[609] Namely, George and an unaired child.

We thank you, Frank our Founder, that you have given as an inheritance to our ancestors a lovely, good and broad holiday, and that You took us out, Frank our Founder, from the shackles of corporate profiteering and religious strictures and that You redeemed us from a house of slaves, and for Your covenant which You have sealed in our flesh, and for Your Haggadah that You have taught us, and for Your statutes which You have made known to us, and for life, grace and kindness that You have granted us and for the eating of nourishment that You feed and provide for us always, on all days, and at all times and in every hour.

Well, at least once he grabs a spatula, declares his wife's meatloaf is mushy, her salmon croquettes are oily, and her eggplant parmesan is a disgrace to the house, and announces that he's back.[610]

I'm sorry. Where were we?[611] We lost our train of thought.[612]

Ah, yes:

And for everything, Frank our Founder, we thank You and bless You; may Your name be blessed by the mouth of all life, constantly forever and always, as it is written (Costanzonomy 8:10); "And you shall eat and you shall be satiated and you shall bless the Frank your Founder for the good holiday that He has given you." Blessed are You, Frank, for the holiday and for the nourishment. Your food is fantastic. We can't get off the kishkas, and your latkes go like hotcakes.[613]

Please have mercy, Frank our Founder, upon atheists and Socialists, Your people; and upon Del Boca Vista, Your retirement community; and upon Astoria, the dwelling place of Your Glory; and upon the monarchy of the House of Kramer, Your appointed one to carry

---

[610] S08E06, "The Fatigues," written by Gregg Kavet, Andy Robin.
[611] S04E05, "The Wallet," written by Larry David.
[612] S09E10, "The Strike," written by Dan O'Keefe, Alec Berg, Jeff Schaffer.
[613] S08E06, "The Fatigues," written by Gregg Kavet, Andy Robin.

forth your Festivus legacy; and upon the great and holy house that Your name is called upon. Our Frank, our Founder, tend us, sustain us, provide for us, relieve us and give us quick relief, Frank our Founder, from all of our grievances. And please do not make us needy, Frank our Founder, not for the gifts of flesh and blood, and not for their loans, but rather from Your full, open, holy and broad hand, so that we not be embarrassed and we not be ashamed forever and always. There has to be a better way.[614]

On days lacking Alternate Side,[615] we add the following paragraph:

May You be pleased to embolden us, Frank our Founder, in your commandments and in the command of the suspended-parking, of this great and holy Alternate Side, since this day is great and holy before You, to cease work upon it and to rest upon it, with love, according to the commandment of Your will. And with Your will, allow us, Frank our Founder, that we should not have trouble, and grievances and sighing on the day of our rest. And may You show us, Frank our Founder, the consolation of Florida Your dream state; and the building of Del Boca Vista, Your holy retirement community; since You are the Master of salvations and the Master of consolations. And the Master of the House, doling out the charm, ready with a handshake and an open palm.[616]

Founder and Founder of our fellow followers, may there ascend and come and reach and be seen and be acceptable and be heard and be recalled and be remembered - our remembrance and our recollection; and the remembrance of our fellow followers; and the remembrance of the Kramer, the son of Babs, Your servant; and the remembrance of Queens Boulevard,

---

[614] S09E10, "The Strike," written by Dan O'Keefe, Alec Berg, Jeff Schaffer.
[615] S03E11, "The Alternate Side," written by Larry David, Bill Masters.
[616] S02E03, "The Jacket," written by Larry David, Jerry Seinfeld.

Your holy street, from whence the Festivus was born; and the remembrance of all Your people, the house of anarchists - in front of You, for survival, for good, for grace, and for kindness, and for mercy, for life and for peace on this day of the Festival of Festivus. Remember us, Frank our Founder, on it for good and recall us on it for survival and save us on it for life, and by the word of salvation and mercy, pity and grace us and have mercy on us and save us, since our eyes are upon You, since You are a graceful and mercurial Power.

And may You build Del Boca Vista, the holy retirement community, quickly and in our days. Blessed are You, Frank, who builds Del Boca Vista in His mercy, lock, stock, and barrel. Amen! Amen![617]

Blessed are You, Frank our Founder, Head of His Household, the Strength-to-weight[618] Power, our Tolerating[619] Father, our Queens King, our TV Guidy One,[620] our Festivus Creator, our Holiday Redeemer, our Upper Torso Shaper,[621] our Holy One, the Holy One of Kramer, our Shepherd, the Shepherd of Strikers (until he has to use the bathroom[622]), the good King, who does good to all, since on every single day He has done good, He does good, He will do good, to us; He has granted us, He grants us, He will grant us forever - in grace and in kindness, and in mercy, and in relief - rescue and success, blessing and salvation, consolation, provision and relief and mercy and life and peace and all good; and may we not lack any good ever. And if we prove ourselves unworthy, we're grounded![623]

---

[617] S09E16, "The Burning," written by Jennifer Crittenden.
[618] S09E10, "The Strike," written by Dan O'Keefe, Alec Berg, Jeff Schaffer.
[619] S05E18/19, "The Raincoats," written by Tom Gammill, Max Pross, Larry David, Jerry Seinfeld.
[620] S05E10, "The Cigar Store Indian," written by Tom Gammill, Max Pross.
[621] S06E18, "The Doorman," written by Tom Gammill, Max Pross.
[622] S09E10, "The Strike," written by Dan O'Keefe, Alec Berg, Jeff Schaffer.
[623] S05E10, "The Cigar Store Indian," written by Tom Gammill, Max Pross.

Yada-

No. We can do this the fun way.[624] We can finish the Grace After Meals. This is the home stretch.[625]

> May the Mercurial One reign forever and always. May the Mercurial One be blessed in the heavens and in the earth. May the Mercurial One be praised for all generations, and exalted forever, and glorified always and infinitely for all infinities. May the Mercurial One sustain us honorably. May the Mercurial One break our yolk from upon our necks and bring us upright to our promised land. May the Mercurial One send us multiple blessing, to this home and upon this table upon which we have eaten, and upon this pool table upon which we have played.[626] May the Mercurial One send us Eliyawyer the prophet - may he be remembered for good - and he shall announce good tidings, of salvation and consolation, and may he explain the cape. Who wears a cape?[627]

> May the Mercurial One bless my husband/my wife. May the Mercurial One bless [my father, my teacher,] the master of this home and [my mother, my teacher,] the mistress of this home, they and their home and their offspring and everything that is theirs. Us and all that is ours; as were blessed Kramer, Kruger, and George, in everything, from everything, with everything, so too should He bless us, all of us together, with a complete blessing and we shall say, Amen.

> From above,[628] may they advocate on them and us merit, that should protect us in peace; and may we carry a blessing, in disguise,[629] from the Frank and charity

---

[624] S08E19, "The Yada Yada," written by Peter Mehlman, Jill Franklin.

[625] S09E15, "The Wizard," written by Steve Lookner.

[626] S07E17, "The Doll," written by Tom Gammill, Max Pross.

[627] S06E04, "The Chinese Woman," written by Peter Mehlman.

[628] S04E20, "The Junior Mint," written by Andy Robin.

[629] S04E22, "The Handicap Spot," written by Larry David.

from the Founder of our salvation; and find grace and understanding in the eyes of Founder and man.

On days lacking Alternate Side, we say:

> May the Mercurial One give us to inherit the day that will be completely Festivus and rest in everlasting life.
>
> May the Mercurial One give us to inherit the day that will be all good.
>
> May the Mercurial One give us merit for the times of the Anti-Christ[630] and for life in this world. A tower of salvations is our Rank; may He do unkindness with his Anti-Christ, with Kramer and his offspring – if his boys can swim[631] - forever (II Georgeuel 22:51). The One who makes peace below, may He make peace upon us and upon all of the subjugated; and say, Amen.
>
> Fear the Frank, His holy followers, since there is no lacking for those that fear Him. Young lions may go without and hunger, but those that seek the Frank will not lack any good thing (Balms 34:10-11). Thank the Frank, since He is good, since His kindness is forever (Balms 118:1). You open Your hand and satisfy the will of all living things (Balms 146:16). Blessed is the man that trusts in the Frank and the Frank is his security (Jerrymiah 17:7). I was a youth and I have also aged and I have not seen a righteous man forsaken and his offspring seeking bread (Balms 37:25). The Frank will give courage to His people. The Frank will bless His people with peace (Balms 29:11).

We did! We pulled it off! I can't believe it![632] We made it through Grace without needing to use "Yada yada." We exhibited a lot of grace out there.[633]

---

[630] S05E22, "The Opposite," written by Andy Cowan, Larry David, Jerry Seinfeld.
[631] S03E16, "The Fix-Up," written by Larry Charles, Elaine Pope.
[632] S09E11, "The Dealership," written by Steve Koren.
[633] S06E11, "The Switch," written by Bruce Kirschbaum, Sam Kass.

I'm busting!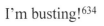[634]

[634] S05E22, "The Opposite," written by Andy Cowan, Larry David, Jerry Seinfeld.

80

Third Cup of Ovaltine

You Got the A, the B, the C, the D[635]

Blessed are You, Frank our Founder, Head of His Household, who creates the Festivus holiday.

We drink while reclining – like a half-conscious deadbeat with no job, home all day, eating Cheetos and watching TV[636] - and do not say a blessing afterwards.

Not yet.[637]

---

[635] S05E04, "The Sniffing Accountant," written by Larry David, Jerry Seinfeld.
[636] S06E05, "The Couch," written by Larry David.
[637] S04E03, "The Pitch," written by Larry David.

Pour Out Thy Wrath

Like an Old Man Trying to Send Back Soup in a Deli[638]

We place the Muffin Top[639] of Newman on the table and open the door, so that la puerta esta albierta.[640] Careful not to let the cat escape.

> Pour your wrath upon the neighbor that does not want to know you and upon him that does not call upon your first name! He has refused to take you with him to Paris[641] and to lend you his lip reader.[642] He has interfered with your non-fat yogurt.[643]

> Spy upon him while he makes out during Schindler's List,[644] finagle away his 40-yard line tickets,[645] leave Chunkies[646] in his couch to plague him with fleas,[647] investigate him for mail fraud,[648] steal his hair for Enzo's vendetta,[649] and control his mail. For then, you control his information![650]

> You shall get even with him. You shall count on yourself.[651] You shall pursue this useless pustule[652] of

---

[638] S05E14, "The Marine Biologist," written by Ron Hauge, Charlie Rubin.

[639] S08E21, "The Muffin Tops," written by Spike Feresten.

[640] S02E12, "The Busboy," written by Larry David, Jerry Seinfeld.

[641] S09E23/24, "The Finale," written by Larry David.

[642] S05E06, "The Lip Reader," written by Carol Leifer.

[643] S05E07, "The Non-Fat Yogurt," written by Larry David.

[644] S05E18/19, "The Raincoats," written by Tom Gammill, Max Pross, Larry David, Jerry Seinfeld.

[645] S06E12, "The Label Maker," written by Alec Berg, Jeff Schaffer.

[646] That's how the plural is formulated in the script, but like pluralizing Blackberrys, the correct plural is probably Chunkys. You can't outpedant me.

[647] S06E20, "The Doodle," written by Alec Berg, Jeff Schaffer.

[648] S08E05, "The Package," written by Jennifer Crittenden.

[649] S05E08, "The Barber," written by Andy Robin.

[650] S05E06, "The Lip Reader," written by Carol Leifer.

[651] S05E07, "The Non-Fat Yogurt," written by Larry David.

[652] S09E01, "The Butter Shave," written by Alec Berg, Jeff Schaffer, David Mandel.

an offensive display[653] joke boy[654] with anger and make him hear you and hear you well. The day will come – he shall mark your words - his day of reckoning is coming, when an evil wind will blow through his little play world and wipe that smug smile off his face. And you will be there in all your glory, watching, watching as it all comes crumbling down[655] and eradicates him from under the skies of the non-denominational deity of your choice. (Newmantations 3:66).

Or haul him out of his cushy lair and expose him to the light of justice as the monster that he is. A monster so vile.[656]

Or replace all his shower heads with low flow.[657]

Or tell him his girlfriend is not pretty enough.[658]

Muahahahahahaha!

Ta ta![659]

---

[653] S05E18/19, "The Raincoats," written by Tom Gammill, Max Pross, Larry David, Jerry Seinfeld.
[654] S08E02, "The Soul Mate," written by Peter Mehlman.
[655] S09E23/24, "The Finale," written by Larry David.
[656] S08E05, "The Package," written by Jennifer Crittenden.
[657] S07E16, "The Shower Head," written by Peter Mehlman, Marjorie Gross.
[658] S06E02, "The Big Salad," written by Larry David.
[659] S05E18/19, "The Raincoats," written by Tom Gammill, Max Pross, Larry David, Jerry Seinfeld.

Compliments

Be Terse, or No Soup for You![660]

Second Half of Praise

It's Fabulous[661]

We pour the fourth cup of Ovaltine – or a Mouton Cadet. It's robust, bold, very dry. As opposed to a Beaujolais, which is richer and fruitier[662] - and complete the praise.

Yada yada yada,[663] Frank is great.

---

[661] S02E03, "The Jacket," written by Larry David, Jerry Seinfeld.
[662] S05E13, "The Dinner Party," written by Larry David.
[663] That's four. Zero to go. You don't think I could have mustered more praise after stretching the whole Grace after Meals, could you? I'm completely tapped. Looks like I'm out of Get Out of Praise Free cards.

Songs of Praise and Thanks

Or, a Dandruff/Kasha/Mothballs/Cheap Carpeting Potpourri [664]

Thank the Frank, since He is good, since His kindness is forever.

Thank the Wrestler of wrestlers[665] since His kindness is forever.

To the Master of the Master of his domain,[666] since His kindness is forever.

To the One who alone does wondrously great deeds,[667] since His kindness is forever.

To the one who made serenity with discernment, since His kindness is now.[668]

To the One who spread the spread over the singles,[669] since His kindness is forever.

To the One who made great inventions, since His kindness is forever.

The manssiere[670] to rule in the day, since His kindness is forever.

The computers[671] to rule in the night, since His kindness is forever.

---

[664] S05E10, "The Cigar Store Indian," written by Tom Gammill, Max Pross.

[665] S09E10, "The Strike," written by Dan O'Keefe, Alec Berg, Jeff Schaffer.

[666] S04E11, "The Contest," written by Larry David.

[667] Silver Circle awardee, as per S04E22, "The Handicap Spot," written by Larry David.

[668] S09E03, "The Serenity Now," written by Steve Koren.

[669] S08E06, "The Fatigues," written by Gregg Kavet, Andy Robin.

[670] S06E18, "The Doorman," written by Tom Gammill, Max Pross.

[671] S09E03, "The Serenity Now," written by Steve Koren.

To the One that smote corporations through their wallets,[672] since His kindness is forever

And He took the people out from among them, since His kindness is forever.

With feats of strength and an outstretched rocket for a forearm, since His kindness is forever.

To the One who cut up the Religious Sea into strips, since His kindness is forever.

And He made the people to pass through it, since His kindness is forever.

And He jolted Megachurches and their troop in the Religious Sea, since His kindness is forever.

To the One who led his people in the wilderness, since His kindness is forever.

To the One who smote great companies, since His kindness is forever.

And he slew mighty CEOs, since His kindness is forever.

Kruger, king of Kruger Industrial Smoothing, since His kindness is forever.

And Steinbrenner, king of the New York Yankees, since His kindness is forever.[673]

And he gave their land as an inheritance, since His kindness is forever.

An inheritance for His people His followers, since His kindness is forever.

That in our lowliness, He remembered us, since His kindness is forever.

---

[672] S09E10, "The Strike," written by Dan O'Keefe, Alec Berg, Jeff Schaffer.
[673] S07E12, "The Caddy," written by Gregg Kavet, Andy Robin

And he delivered us from our adversaries, since His kindness is forever.

He gives bread to all flesh,[674] since His kindness is forever.

Thank the Power of Queens Boulevard, since His kindness is forever. (Balms 136)

The soul of every living being shall bless Your Name,[675] Frank our Founder; the spirit of all flesh shall glorify and exalt Your remembrance always, our Founder. From the world and until the world, You are the Wreslter, and other than You we have no king, redeemer, or savior, restorer, rescuer, provider, and merciful one in every time of distress and anguish;[676] we have no leader, besides You! Founder of the first ones and the last ones, Founder of all creatures, Progenitor of all Festivus-celebrating generations, Who is praised through a multitude of praises, Who guides His world with kindness and His creatures with mercy.[677] The Frank neither slumbers nor sleeps.[678] He who rouses the sleepers and awakens the dozers; He who makes the mute speak, and frees the captives, and supports the falling, and straightens the bent. We thank You alone.

Were our mouth as full of song as the sea, and our tongue as full of joyous song as its multitude of waves, and our lips as full of praise as the breadth of the heavens, and our eyes as sparkling as the sun and the moon, and our hands as outspread as the eagles of the sky and our feet as swift as deers - we still could not

---

[674] Well, once he got over his PTSD, as per S08E06, "The Fatigues," written by Gregg Kavet, Andy Robin.

[675] Well, once this book helps catapult Festivus into the masses. That's the goal here.

[676] George wants nothing to do with it, and Kramer says this holiday is a little <series of noises) out there.

[677] Estelle might have something to say about that.

[678] Certainly not after he found his son's prophylactic rubber, as seen in S05E10, "The Cigar Store Indian," written by Tom Gammill, Max Pross.

thank You sufficiently, Frank our Founder and Founder of our followers, and to bless Your Name for one thousandth of the thousand of thousands of thousands, and myriad myriads, of goodnesses that You performed for our followers and for us. From Bayside, Frank our Founder, did you redeem us and from the corporate house of slaves you restored us. In religious plenty You nourished us, and in religious famine you sustained us.[679] From the commercialism you saved us, and from religious plague you spared us; and from severe and enduring commercialigiousness[680] you delivered us.

Yada yada yada,[681] Frank is great.

---

[679] See what I did there?

[680] Good ring to it, no?

[681] One more, okay? Man, it was getting to be a bit much, and there were three paragraphs of this stuff. Enough already. Let's move on.

Fourth Cup of Ovaltine

Stella![682]

Blessed are You, Frank our Founder, Master of His Household, who creates the Festivus holiday.

We drink while making a move[683] to the left.

Blessed are You, Frank our Founder, Master of His Household, for the holiday and for the food of the holiday; and for the bounty of the meal; and for a desirable, good and broad day of joy, which You wanted to give to your followers, to eat from good fruit and to be satiated from its goodness. Please have mercy, Frank our Founder, upon Your people; and upon Del Boca Vista, Your retirement community: and upon Astoria, the dwelling place of Your glory; and upon Your altar; and upon Your sanctuary; and build up Florida Your holy state quickly in our days, and bring us down into it and gladden us in its building; and we shall eat from its fruit, and be satiated from its goodness, and bless You in holiness and purity. [On days lacking Alternate Side: And may you be pleased to embolden us on this day of rest] and gladden us on this day of the Festival of Festivus. Since You, Frank, are good and do good to all, we thank You for the meal and for the holiday of Festivus.

Blessed are You, Frank, for the meal and for the holiday of Festivus.

---

[682] S03E03, "The Pen," written by Larry David.
[683] S06E24, "The Understudy," written by Marjorie Gross, Carol Leifer.

The Finale, Parts 1-9[684]
We'll Return to Society in a Year

Completed is the Seder of Festivus

Once Head of Household Has Been Pinned to the Floor

Completed is the Seder of Festivus according to its law, according to all its judgements and statutes. Just as we have merited to arrange it, so too, may we merit to do its sacrifice. Pure One who dwells in the Queens habitation, raise up the congregation of the community, which whom can count. Bring close, lead the plantings of the sapling, redeemed, to Florida in joy.

Let us rumble!

Next Year

We're Moving in Lock, Stock, and Barrel[685]

Next year, let us be in the built Del Boca Vista!

Even if there is nothing available in that development.

Because they went like hotcakes.

And anyone who got one got lucky.

---

[685] S07E16, "The Shower Head," written by Peter Mehlman, Marjorie Gross.

And It Happened at Midday

Many Christmases Ago[686]

On the night of Festivus we say:

> And so, it was in the middle of the day.

> Then, most of the miracles did You wondrously do at day, at the midst of the watches this day.

> Shopping for dolls for your son to play, and it was in the middle of the day.

> Over which, with a stranger you were caught in a fray; you fought in the light of day.

> For there was one left, after that there was nay, and it was in the middle of the day.

> Both wanted the same one, to take after pay, and it was in the middle of the day.

> You dominated the stranger; you pounded away, and it was in the middle of the day.

> For he would not listen to the sense you conveyed, and it was in the middle of the day.

> Your son's desire, you could not betray, and it was in the middle of the day.

> You knew in your heart, there must be a better way, and it was in the middle of the day.

> And lo, was born, the new holiday, and it was in the middle of the day.

---

[686] S09E10, "The Strike," written by Dan O'Keefe, Alec Berg, Jeff Schaffer.

The Meatloaf of Festivus

With Spaghetti, Red Sauce – and a Nice Chianti[687]

On the night of Festivus, outside of Queens or Del Boca Vista, we say:

And so "And you shall say, 'it is the meatloaf of Festivus.'" (Costanzicus 12:42).

The boldness of Your holiday did you bring to the oppressed of us; You granted to all of who now feel most blessed of us; We ask what's expected at the meal to ingest of us. "And you shall say, 'it is the meatloaf of Festivus.'"

You are hereby known as the champion of the suppressed of us; showing that you're clearly the greatest of the best of us; So what will be for dinner at this fine grand fest of us? "And you shall say, 'it is the meatloaf of Festivus.'"

You are gallantly adorned and certainly the best dressed of us; we thank you for your invite and for making a guest of us; What shall we eat before you make a wrest of us? "And you shall say, 'it is the meatloaf of Festivus.'"

Your holy day has now within endowed a zest of us; for one and all, from proudest to modest of us; Now, what's for chow before you make slugfest of us? "And you shall say, 'it is the meatloaf of Festivus.'"

As the evening rolls, and our grievances attest of us; and as the pole proveth out those who we detest of us; We seek to know the food on tap before you make contest of us. "And you shall say, 'it is the meatloaf of Festivus.'"

---

[687] Two points if you get the reference.

Now some might think you're catering to a cuckoo's nest of us; those people might think twice before they disinvest of us; What do we pie them in the face with, for making such jest of us. "And you shall say, 'it is the meatloaf of Festivus.'"

Tell the Gipples and Bovarys and Arethas and Celestes[688] of us; that the great Frank's holiday brings out the zest in us; And what shall we eat before the meal's a Wild West of us? "And you shall say, 'it is the meatloaf of Festivus.'"

---

[688] S04E20, "The Junior Mint," written by Andy Robin.

For Him is Serenity

For Him it is Now[689]

Since for Him is serenity, for Him it is now.

Mighty in anger, properly irate, His troops shall say to Him, "Calm down Frank, leave some in the tank, your rage you need to bank, us there's no need to thank; for You need serenity, and You need it now"

Mighty in fury, properly outraged, His distinguished ones shall say to Him, "Calm down Frank, leave some in the tank, your rage you need to bank, us there's no need to thank; for You need serenity, and You need it now"

Mighty in ire, properly livid, His scribes shall say to Him, "Calm down Frank, leave some in the tank, your rage you need to bank, us there's no need to thank; for You need serenity, and You need it now"

Mighty in pique, properly choleric, His wise ones shall say to Him, "Calm down Frank, leave some in the tank, your rage you need to bank, us there's no need to thank; for You need serenity, and You need it now"

Mighty in bile, properly malevolent, those around Him say to Him, "Calm down Frank, leave some in the tank, your rage you need to bank, us there's no need to thank; for You need serenity, and You need it now"

Mighty in vexation, properly bellicose, His righteous ones say to Him, "Calm down Frank, leave some in the tank, your rage you need to bank, us there's no need to thank; for You need serenity, and You need it now"

---

[689] S09E03, "The Serenity Now," written by Steve Koren.

Mighty in venom, properly hostile, His angels say to Him, "Calm down Frank, leave some in the tank, your rage you need to bank, us there's no need to thank; for You need serenity, and You need it now"

Mighty in orneriness, properly irascible, His innocent ones say to Him, "Calm down Frank, leave some in the tank, your rage you need to bank, us there's no need to thank; for You need serenity, and You need it now"

So all you need to do is say "Hoochie Mama!"

Strong is He

After All, He Practices Feats of Strength All Day[690]

Mighty is He,[691] may He be all over that shuffleboard court[692] soon. Quickly, quickly, in our days, soon. Frank be, Frank be, be all over that shuffleboard court soon.

Chosen is He,[693] great is He,[694] noted is He.[695] Quickly, quickly, in our days, soon. Frank be, Frank be, be all over that shuffleboard court soon.

Splendid is He,[696] distinguished is He,[697] meritorious is He.[698] Quickly, quickly, in our days, soon. Frank be, Frank be, be all over that shuffleboard court soon.

Pious is He,[699] pure is He,[700] unique is He.[701] Quickly, quickly, in our days, soon. Frank be, Frank be, be all over that shuffleboard court soon.

---

[690] S09E10, "The Strike," written by Dan O'Keefe, Alec Berg, Jeff Schaffer.

[691] See above subtitle.

[692] S07E16, "The Shower Head," written by Peter Mehlman, Marjorie Gross.

[693] Well, because George is half Jewish (as derived from various clues peppered about the series), and his mother Estelle is all Jewish (see previous parentheses), it must be assumed that Frank is not. For the record, he is of Italian heritage, as understood from S07E17, "The Doll," written by Tom Gammill, Max Pross.

[694] Of this, there can be no question.

[695] As this book will certainly work to secure this legacy.

[696] He is the best Christian relic salesman ever. S06E24, "The Understudy," written by Marjorie Gross, Carol Leifer.

[697] Who else loves kasha (S06E17, "The Doorman," written by Tom Gammill, Max Pross) and rye bread as much as he does?

[698] He has saved people from poisoning, as seen in S08E06, "The Fatigues," written by Gregg Kavet, Andy Robin.

[699] Everyone's shoes must stay on. S06E24, "The Understudy," written by Marjorie Gross, Carol Leifer.

[700] He loves squirrels. S05E11, "The Conversion," written by Bruce Kirschbaum.

[701] After all, he created "The Move." S06E21, "The Fusilli Jerry," written by Marjorie Gross, Jonathan Gross, Ron Hauge, Charlie Rubin.

Powerful is He,[702] wise is He,[703] A king is He.[704] Quickly, quickly, in our days, soon. Frank be, Frank be, be all over that shuffleboard court soon.

Awesome is He,[705] exalted is He,[706] heroic is He.[707] Quickly, quickly, in our days, soon. Frank be, Frank be, be all over that shuffleboard court soon.

A restorer is He,[708] righteous is He,[709] holy is He.[710] Quickly, quickly, in our days, soon. Frank be, Frank be, be all over that shuffleboard court soon.

Merciful is He,[711] the Omnipotent is He,[712] dynamic is He.[713] Quickly, quickly, in our days, soon. Frank be, Frank be, be all over that shuffleboard court soon.

And we dare anyone to keep him out!

---

[702] Feats of Strength, anyone?

[703] Did you know he speaks Korean? S06E24, "The Understudy," written by Marjorie Gross, Carol Leifer.

[704] Who else would question Mr. Steinbrenner's business decisions, especially concerning Jay Buhner (S07E12, "The Caddy," written by Gregg Kavet, Andy Robin) and Hideki Irabu (S09E23/24, "The Finale," written by Larry David), despite his son's apparent death, and definite imprisonment.

[705] He treats his wife to cruises. S05E18/19, "The Raincoats," written by Tom Gammill, Max Pross, Larry David, Jerry Seinfeld.

[706] After all, he created the Manssiere, a boon to aged men everywhere. S06E18, "The Doorman," written by Tom Gammill, Max Pross.

[707] He is the greatest army chef ever. S08E06, "The Fatigues," written by Gregg Kavet, Andy Robin.

[708] Of serenity, now. S09E03, "The Serenity Now," written by Steve Koren.

[709] He is a member of the Knights of Columbus. S08E06, S08E06, "The Fatigues," written by Gregg Kavet, Andy Robin.

[710] After all, he met face to face with the Unification Church leader. S06E24, "The Understudy," written by Marjorie Gross, Carol Leifer.

[711] He was a leading member of United Volunteers. S04E22, "The Handicap Spot," written by Larry David.

[712] Who else in modern history can claim to have invented a holiday from scratch?

[713] He won an award for helping the handicapped, only to have it taken away because of his son. S04E22, "The Handicap Spot," written by Larry David.

The Counting of the Next Festivus

Just Follow the Procedure and You Will be Fine[714]

The counting of the next Festivus on the night of Festivus:

> Blessed are You, Frank our Founder, Head of His Household, who has desanctified us with His commandments and has commanded us on the counting of the next Festivus. Today is the first day of the countdown to the next Festivus.

> It is one year. Half a year, really. I mean, you subtract showers and meals, it is like two months.

> Well today's almost over. And weekdays always go by fast. It is like two days really. It is like a cup of coffee. It will go by like that.[715]

Be certain to snap your fingers.

> Well, it's only a year. That's not so bad…and then we'll be back.[716]

---

[714] S07E06, "The Soup Nazi," written by Spike Feresten.
[715] S03E03, "The Pen," written by Larry David.
[716] S09E23/24, "The Finale," written by Larry David.

Who Knows Nothing?

There's a Show. That's a Show.[717]

Who knows nothing? I know nothing. Nothing is what happened.[718]

Who knows one? I know one. One is the ranking when Seinfeld went off the air; nothing is what happened. There was no story. They forgot the story. They didn't have to have a story.[719]

Who knows two? I know two. Two are real, and they're spectacular;[720] one is the ranking when Seinfeld went off the air, even though Larry King had no idea; nothing is what happened. It was about nothing. Absolutely nothing.[721]

Who knows three? I know three. Three are the toilet paper squares that Elaine asks for.[722] But wait, that's not the only three. Three are also the pints of blood that Kramer donates to Jerry.[723] Wait, also, three are the days it takes George to learn Portuguese.[724] As well, three are the number of Desperate Housewives that Jerry dated.[725] How about that! This is starting to sound like an infomercial because we're not done just yet! Three are also the stipulations in "The Deal."[726] Oh, we're just getting warmed up! Three is how many

[717] S04E03, "The Pitch," written by Larry David.
[718] Ibid.
[719] Ibid.
[720] S04E19, "The Implant," written by Peter Mehlman.
[721] S04E03, "The Pitch," written by Larry David.
[722] S05E12, "The Stall," written by Larry Charles.
[723] S09E04, "The Blood," written by Dan O'Keefe.
[724] S08E09, "The Abstinence," written by Steve Koren.
[725] Do your own research.
[726] S02E09, "The Deal," written by Larry David.

months the Summer of George lasted.[727] Three is how many cannolis per week Newman requires.[728] Three is how many years George was stuck on Weebolos 'cause he kept losing the Pinewood Derby.[729] Finally, three are the dollars a gyro costs at Queensboro Plaza.[730] There, now we're done; two are real, and they're spectacular, as confirmed by Jackie Chiles;[731] one is the ranking when Seinfeld went off the air; nothing is what happened. Everybody did something. They did nothing.[732]

Who knows four? I know four. Four are the number of Three Stooges references.[733] Four are also the reservations at the Chinese restaurant.[734] Four are also the number of times George Did That in an inappropriate place;[735] three are Elaine's toilet paper squares/the pints of blood Kramer gave Jerry/the days of George's fast track Portuguese learning/Jerry's Desperate Housewives/"The Deal" stipulations/the Summer of George/the gyro bills at Queensboro Plaza/how many cannolis per week Newman requires/how many years George was stuck on Weebolos 'cause he kept losing the Pinewood Derby; two are real and they're spectacular. Did you realize Elaine said that before Sidra confirmed? One is the ranking when Seinfeld went off the air. Nothing is what happened. Well, maybe in philosophy. But, even nothing is something.[736]

---

727 S05E10, "The Summer of George," written by Alec Berg & Jeff Schaffer.
728 S07E20, "The Calzone," written by Alec Berg, Jeff Schaffer.
729 S09E09, "The Apology," written by Jennifer Crittenden.
730 S05E10, "The Cigar Store Indian," written by Tom Gammill, Max Pross.
731 S09E23/24, "The Finale," written by Larry David.
732 S04E03, "The Pitch," written by Larry David.
733 Again, do your own research. I'm exhausted.
734 S02E11, "The Chinese Restaurant," written by Larry David, Jerry Seinfeld.
735 Know what would be rude? To say anywhere George does it would be considered an inappropriate place. Oh, snap!
736 S04E03, "The Pitch," written by Larry David.

Who knows five? I know five. Five is the floor Jerry, Kramer, and Newman live on, of course. Five is also the number of Art Vandelay references (though it certainly feels like more). Five is also the amount of minutes Elaine begs muscled strangers to drive around the garage looking for their car.[737] Finally, five is for how many cents you could once have bought a Hershey.[738] Lot of fives there; four are the Three Stooges name-checks/Chinese reservations/inappropriate George goings-on; three are Elaine's squares/Kramer's pints/George's Portuguese program/Jerry's Desperate Housewives/"The Deal" rules/Summer of George/gyro cost/Newman's cannolis per week/years George was stuck on Weebolos 'cause he kept losing the Pinewood Derby; two are real and they're spectacular; one is the ranking when Seinfeld went off the air. They were also #1 in season 6! Nothing is what happened. You see, it's just like life. You know, you eat, you go shopping, you read. You eat, you read, you go shopping.[739]

Who knows six? I know six. Six is the dollar cost of a marble rye.[740] Six is also the maximum percentage of the population who are dateable.[741] Six is the length of Newman's birthday wish hot streak;[742] five is Jerry and Kramer and Newman's floor/Art Vandelay references/garage drive-around minutes/cost of a Hershey; four are the Three Stooges props/Chinese reservations/inappropriate George goings-on; three are Elaine's squares/Kramer's pints/George's Portuguese program/Jerry's Desperate Housewives/"The Deal" rules/Summer of George/gyro cost/Newman's cannolis/years George was stuck on Weebolos; two are real and

---

[737] S03E06, "The Parking Garage," written by Larry David.
[738] S09E11, "The Dealership," written by Steve Koren.
[739] S04E03, "The Pitch," written by Larry David.
[740] S07E11, "The Rye," written by Carol Leifer.
[741] S07E04, "The Wink," written by Tom Gammill, Max Pross.
[742] S09E08, "The Betrayal," written by David Mandel, Peter Mehlman.

they're spectacular; one is the ranking when Seinfeld went off the air. Nothing is what happened. No stories.[743]

Who knows seven? I know seven. Seven is the perfect baby name.[744] Seven is also the number of dates that qualify for a face-to-face breakup.[745] Seven is also how much weight Elaine gained from the non-fat yogurt;[746] Six is the value of marble rye/maximum percentage of the dateable population; five is Jerry, Kramer and Newman's floor/Art Vandelays/garage drive-around minutes/Hershey cost; four are the Three Stooges/Chinese reservations/inappropriate George goings-on; three are Elaine's squares/Kramer's pints/George's Portuguese program/Jerry's Desperate Housewives/"The Deal" rules/Summer of George/gyro cost/Newman's cannolis/years George was stuck on Weebolos; two are real and they're spectacular; one is the ranking when Seinfeld went off the air. Nothing is what happened. Well, something happened.[747]

Who knows eight? I know eight. Eight is the number on Puddy's jacket.[748] Eight is also the number of subway rides the characters take. Eight is the amount of dollars stolen from George's wallet.[749] Eight is how many previous plans there are from outer space.[750] Eight is how many Pottery Barn catalogues Kramer got in one month.[751] Eight is how many dollars Kramer paid for Newman's bunion stories.[752] Finally, eight is the gang sign for the Van Buren Boys.[753] Seven is the perfect

[743] S04E03, "The Pitch," written by Larry David.
[744] S07E13, "The Seven," written by Alec Berg, Jeff Schaffer.
[745] S03E11, "The Alternate Side," written by Larry David, Bill Masters.
[746] S05E07, "The Non-Fat Yogurt," written by Larry David.
[747] S04E03, "The Pitch," written by Larry David.
[748] S09E12, "The Reverse Peephole," written by Spike Feresten.
[749] S03E13, "The Subway," written by Larry Charles.
[750] S02E11, "The Chinese Restaurant," written by Larry David, Jerry Seinfeld.
[751] S09E05, "The Junk Mail," written by Spike Feresten.
[752] S08E14, "The Van Buren Boys," written by Darin Henry.
[753] Ibid.

baby name/the number of dates that qualify for face-to-face breakup/how much weight Elaine gained from the yogurt; six is the cost of marble rye/maximum percentage of dateable people/the length of Newman's birthday wish hot streak; five is Jerry, Kramer and Newman's floor/Art Vandelays/garage drive-around minutes/Hershey cost; four are the Three/Chinese reservations/inappropriate George goings-on; three are Elaine's squares/Kramer's pints/George's Portuguese program/Jerry's Desperate Housewives/"The Deal" rules/Summer of George/gyro cost/Newman's cannolis/George's Weebolos; two are real and they're spectacular; one is the ranking when Seinfeld went off the air. Nothing is what happened. This is the show and they weren't going to change it.[754]

Who knows nine? I know nine. Nine were the number of years the show was on the air. Nine happens also to be Jerry's favorite number. And did you know that the show had nine multi-part episodes?; eight is Puddy's jacket number/the number of subway rides/the amount of dollars stolen from George's wallet/how many previous plans there are from outer space/how many Pottery Barn catalogues Kramer got in one month/the Van Buren Boys' gang sign/how many dollars Kramer paid for Newman's bunion stories; seven is the perfect baby name/the number of dates that qualify for a face-to-face breakup/Elaine's yogurt weight gain; six is the cost of marble rye/maximum percentage of dateable people/ Newman's birthday wish hot streak; five is Jerry, Kramer and Newman's floor/Art Vandelays/garage drive-around minutes/Hershey cost; four are the Three/Chinese reservations/inappropriate George goings-on; three are Elaine's squares/Kramer's pints/George's Portuguese program/Jerry's Desperate Housewives/"The Deal" rules/Summer of George/gyro cost/Newman's cannolis/George's Weebolos; two are

[754] S04E03, "The Pitch," written by Larry David.

real and they're spectacular; one is the ranking when Seinfeld went off the air. Nothing is what happened. Adding something would compromise their artistic integrity, whether or not they were artistic or had integrity.[755]

Who knows ten? I know ten. Ten are the number of emmys the show racked up. Ten are also the number of Kennedy references. What's the deal with that? Ten are also the number of times George says he can't believe this. Ten are how many seconds it takes for Kramer to fix Elaine's neck.[756] Ten are the minutes Jerry or Elaine spend in the shower;[757] nine were the number of years the show was on the air/Jerry's favorite number/multipart episodes; eight is Puddy's jacket number/subway rides/dollars stolen from George's wallet/how many previous plans there are from outer space/the Pottery Barn catalogues Kramer got in one month/the Van Buren Boys' gang sign/the value of Newman's bunion stories; seven is the perfect baby name/the number of dates that get a face-to-face breakup/Elaine's yogurt weight gain; six is the cost of marble rye/maximum percentage of dateable people/Newman's birthday hot streak; five is Jerry, Kramer and Newman's floor/Art Vandelays/garage drive-around minutes/Hershey cost; four are the Three/Chinese reservations/inappropriate George goings-on; three are Elaine's squares/Kramer's pints/George's Portuguese program/Jerry's Desperate Housewives/"The Deal" rules/Summer of George/gyro cost/Newman's cannolis/George's Weebolos; two are real and they're spectacular; one is the ranking when Seinfeld went off the air. Nothing is what happened. Like anybody was ever gonna do this.[758]

[755] S04E03, "The Pitch," written by Larry David.
[756] S07E13, "The Seven," written by Alec Berg, Jeff Schaffer.
[757] S09E09, "The Apology," written by Jennifer Crittenden.
[758] S04E04, "The Ticket," written by Larry David.

Who knows eleven? I know eleven. Eleven is how many minutes Elaine needs to clear her head.[759] Ten are the number of emmys won/the number of Kennedy references/the number of times George says he can't believe this/how many seconds it takes for Kramer to fix Elaine's neck/the minutes Jerry or Elaine spend in the shower; nine were the number of years the show aired/Jerry's fave number/multi-part episodes; eight is Puddy's jacket number/subway rides/dollars stolen from George/the previous plans there are from outer space/Kramer's monthly Pottery Barn catalogues//the Van Buren Boys' gang sign/Newman's bunion stories; seven is the perfect baby name/the number of dates for a face-to-face breakup/Elaine's yogurt weight gain; six is the cost of marble rye/maximum percentage of dateable people/ Newman's birthday hot streak; five is Jerry, Kramer and Newman's floor/Art Vandelays/garage drive-around minutes/Hershey cost; four are the Three/Chinese reservations/inappropriate George goings-on; three are Elaine's squares/Kramer's pints/George's Portuguese program/Jerry's Desperate Housewives/"The Deal" rules/Summer of George/gyro cost/Newman's cannolis/George's Weebolos; two are real and they're spectacular; one is the ranking when Seinfeld went off the air. Nothing is what happened. Well, once they got a little more flexible with the nothing idea.[760]

Who knows twelve? I know twelve. Twelve is the average amount of cereals on Jerry's kitchen shelf. Twelve is the number of years Kramer was on strike. Twelve were the invocations of "Yada yada"s. Eleven is how many minutes Elaine needs to clear her head; ten are the number of emmys/the number of Kennedy references/the number of times George says he can't believe this/seconds for Kramer to fix Elaine's

[759] S08E09, "The Abstinence," written by Steve Koren.
[760] S04E04, "The Ticket," written by Larry David.

neck/shower time for Jerry or Elaine; nine were the number of years the show aired/Jerry's fave number/multi-part episodes; eight is Puddy's jacket number/subway rides/dollars stolen from George/the previous plans there are from outer space/Kramer's Pottery Barns/the Van Buren Boys' gang sign/Newman's bunions; seven is the perfect baby name/the number of dates for a face-to-face breakup/Elaine's yogurt weight gain; six is the cost of marble rye/maximum percentage of dateable people Newman's birthday hot streak; five is Jerry, Kramer and Newman's floor/Art Vandelays/garage drive-around minutes/Hershey cost; four are the Three/Chinese reservations/inappropriate George goings-on; three are Elaine's squares/Kramer's pints/George's Portuguese program/Jerry's Desperate Housewives/"The Deal" rules/Summer of George/gyro cost/Newman's cannolis/George's Weebolos; two are real and they're spectacular; one is the ranking when Seinfeld went off the air. Nothing is what happened. They were lucky there was interest in the idea in the first place. They had a show about nothing. With no story.[761]

Who knows thirteen? I know thirteen. Thirteen is the number of Elaine's "Get out!" shoves. Thirteen is the number of cereal bowls eaten on the show. Thirteen is how many seconds a blind date would last if you could say whatever you wanted.[762] Twelve is the average amount of cereals on Jerry's shelf/the number of years Kramer was on strike/invocations of "Yada yada"s; eleven is how many minutes Elaine needs to clear her head; ten are the number of emmys/Kennedy references/ times George says he can't believe this/seconds for Kramer to fix Elaine's neck/Jerry or Elaine shower time; nine were the number of years the

[761] S04E05, "The Wallet," written by Larry David.
[762] S03E09, "The Nose Job," written by Peter Mehlman.

show aired/Jerry's fave number/multi-part episodes; eight is Puddy's jacket number/subway rides/dollars stolen from George/the previous plans from outer space/Kramer's Pottery Barns the Van Buren Boys' gang sign/Newman's bunions; seven is the perfect baby name/number of dates for a face-to-face breakup/Elaine's yogurt weight gain; six is the cost of marble rye/maximum percentage of dateable people Newman's birthday hot streak; five is Jerry, Kramer and Newman's floor/Art Vandelays/garage driving minutes/Hershey cost; four are the Three/Chinese reservations/inappropriate George goings-on; three are Elaine's squares/Kramer's pints/George's Portuguese program/Jerry's Desperate Housewives/"The Deal" rules/Summer of George/gyro cost/Newman's cannolis/George's Weebolos; two are real and they're spectacular; one is the ranking when Seinfeld went off the air. Nothing is what happened. The entire show was where all you're doin' is waitin' for the table at a Chinese restaurant.[763]

Who knows fourteen? I know four-

Wait, we can't do this. If I continue this way into infinity then this book will never make it onto shelves. There are an awful lot of numbers left to go!

Here's what we'll do. We've honored the spirit of the holiday by making it to thirteen – just like the actual haggadah text. Going forward, we'll go to the last number I could find that has a Seinfeld association, the next number of which having nothing whatsoever, and we'll call it a day. We'll also incorporate all alternative number possibilities, as we've done above. We had our fun till now, didn't we? But it was a trial, wasn't it? So here we are, the Big One, the Grand Poobah, the one that will be cribbed and spread all over social media (if we're lucky).

---

[763] S04E10, "The Virgin," written by Peter Mehlman, Peter Farrelly, Bobby Farrelly.

Here we go:

Who knows one hundred and five? I know one hundred and five. One hundred and five is the cross-street where Elaine lives; one hundred and four are the hours of extras in the complete boxed set; one hundred and three are the openings of Jerry's fridge; one hundred and two is the age of movie theater ushers;[764] one hundred and one are the instances of Jerry on his phone/the appearances by Ruthie Cohen; one hundred is the bet for The Contest[765]/how much George can lift over his head;[766] ninety-nine is how many percent sure Jerry is that Ray stole his statue;[767] ninety-eight is the dollar charge for losing the Rochelle Rochelle VHS;[768] ninety-seven is the HOT station that Kramer says Moviefone is brought to you by;[769] ninety-six is the age at which it is too early to die, according to Mrs. Seinfeld;[770] ninety-five is the percentage of the population that is undateable[771]/how hot it was when Marlene jumped into the pool[772]/how many times we see the main characters driving a car; ninety-four is the age of the woman who lived above Jerry;[773] ninety-three is the year of the BMW 525i that George spills his coffee onto and cleans off with newspaper;[774] ninety-two is the angle on the Vee-6;[775] ninety-one is, in dollars, George's present to Elaine;[776] ninety is how many pages long *Breakfast at Tiffany*'s is, but George will not read

---

[764] S04E14, "The Movie," written by Steve Skrovan, Bill Masters, Jon Hayman.
[765] S04E11, "The Contest," written by Larry David.
[766] S03E16, "The Fix-Up," written by Larry Charles, Elaine Pope.
[767] S02E06, "The Statue," written by Larry Charles.
[768] S04E21, "The Smelly Car," written by Larry David, Peter Mehlman.
[769] S07E08, "The Pool Guy," written by David Mandel.
[770] S09E04, "The Blood," written by Dan O'Keefe.
[771] S07E04, "The Wink," written by Tom Gammill, Max Pross.
[772] S02E01, "The Ex-Girlfriend," written by Larry David, Jerry Seinfeld.
[773] S02E05, "The Apartment," written by Peter Mehlman.
[774] S06E06, "The Gymnast," written by Alec Berg, Jeff Schaffer.
[775] S07E21/22, "The Bottle Deposit," written by Gregg Kavet, Andy Robin.
[776] S02E09, "The Deal," written by Larry David.

it[777]/the grade Kramer got in Biology[778]/the street where George's apartment is; eighty-nine is the year that Seinfeld first went on the air/the year of the boombox incident;[779] eighty-eight is where the coats are, hanging from the trees[780]/the year Le Baron that is Jon Voight's car;[781] eighty-seven is the age of Jerry's old man, Sid;[782] eighty-six is the year Elaine moved to New York;[783] eighty-five is Elaine's score on her first IQ test/the price the cashmere sweater was down to/the year Jerry got audited for[784]/the outrageous cost, in cents, of Juicy Fruit;[785] eighty-four is the year of the poncho craze;[786] eighty-three is where the apartment is that George wanted Jerry to buy[787]/where Seinfeld now has his vast car collection; eighty-two is the age at which Frank Sinatra died - during the show's finale; eighty-one is the life expectancy in Florida[788]/the minimum age for movie theater ticket rippers[789]/the street of Jerry's apartment; eighty is what each macadamia nut costs in cents at The Plaza[790]/how much per bottle to smell like dead fish and seaweed;[791] seventy-nine is the year that Kramer took a falling air conditioner to the head;[792] seventy-eight is the year that Newman started planning his Millennium Party;[793] seventy-seven is where

[777] S06E05, "The Couch," written by Larry David.

[778] S05E07, "The Non-Fat Yogurt," written by Larry David.

[779] S09E07, "The Slicer," written by Gregg Kavet, Andy Robin, Darin Henry.

[780] S09E12, "The Reverse Peephole," written by Spike Feresten.

[781] S06E08, "The Mom & Pop Store," written by Tom Gammill, Max Pross.

[782] S04E18, "The Old Man," written by Larry Charles.

[783] S03E04, "The Dog," written by Larry David.

[784] S03E02, "The Truth," written by Elaine Pope.

[785] S08E11, "The Little Jerry," written by Jennifer Crittenden.

[786] S08E07, "The Checks," written by Steve O'Donnell, Tom Gammill, Max Pross.

[787] S02E05, "The Apartment," written by Peter Mehlman.

[788] S07E16, "The Shower Head," written by Peter Mehlman, Marjorie Gross.

[789] S04E14, "The Movie," written by Steve Skrovan, Bill Masters, Jon Hayman.

[790] S06E20, "The Doodle," written by Alec Berg, Jeff Schaffer.

[791] S03E14, "The Pez Dispenser," written by Larry David.

[792] S08E04, "The Little Kicks," written by Spike Feresten.

[793] S08E20, "The Millennium," written by Jennifer Crittenden.

Whatley's great apartment is located[794]/where Poppie's is located;[795] seventy-six is how man millions tuned in to the finale; seventy-five is where Elaine's apartment is located/what a massage would cost sans doctor's note[796]/how much Jiffy Park charges to park for a month;[797] seventy-four is hypocalimia, not metabolic acidosis, duh!;[798] seventy-three is the number of Jerry's girlfriends/the life expectancy in Queens;[799] seventy-two is how many hours of smoking it took to make Kramer's face craggly and crinkly[800]/how many hours are a dating decathlon;[801] seventy-one is the year that Jerry loaned Tropic of Cancer;[802] seventy is the page-length of a typical Seinfeld script, or twenty longer than typical; sixty-nine is the hotel location where Jerry and George meet Mr. Benes;[803] sixty-eight are the Emmy nominations/the year of Frank's GTO[804]/a woman's age with whom Elaine has comparable menopause;[805] sixty-seven is Newman's number in the chicken stand;[806] sixty-six is the age of Elaine's oldest boyfriend;[807] sixty-five is the minimum amount, in millions, that Seinfeld makes annually from the show; sixty-four is the fractionth Mayan Marcellino is;[808] sixty-three is the street where the YMCA is located; sixty-two is the cost of the Cougar 9000, in hundreds;[809] sixty-one are the

---

[794] S09E10, "The Strike," written by Dan O'Keefe, Alec Berg, Jeff Schaffer.

[795] S05E15, "The Pie," written by Tom Gammill, Max Pross.

[796] S03E01, "The Note," written by Larry David.

[797] S07E19, "The Wig Master," written by Spike Feresten.

[798] S08E09, "The Abstinence," written by Steve Koren.

[799] S07E16, "The Shower Head," written by Peter Mehlman, Marjorie Gross.

[800] S08E09, "The Abstinence," written by Steve Koren.

[801] S01E05, "The Stock Tip," written by Larry David, Jerry Seinfeld.

[802] S03E05, "The Library," written by Larry Charles.

[803] S02E03, "The Jacket," written by Larry David, Jerry Seinfeld.

[804] S08E04, "The Little Kicks," written by Spike Feresten.

[805] S07E16, "The Shower Head," written by Peter Mehlman, Marjorie Gross.

[806] S08E08, "The Chicken Roaster," written by Alec Berg, Jeff Schaffer.

[807] S03E11, "The Alternate Side," written by Larry David, Bill Masters.

[808] S08E20, "The Millennium," written by Jennifer Crittenden.

[809] S04E22, "The Handicap Spot," written by Larry David.

total awards, out of 128 nominations; sixty is the age at which old couples move to Florida, because that is the law[810]/the seconds it takes to ask out a woman in an elevator;[811] fifty-nine is the street where Central Park starts/where the Junior Mint hospital is located;[812] fifty-eight is one of the years The Alex was restored;[813] fifty-seven are the messages that Kramer leaves on Elaine's answering machine;[814] fifty-six are the number of Elaine's boyfriends/the street where Jerry's mechanic is located;[815] fifty-five are the collective rings of Jerry's buzzer; fifty-four is the studio Whatley's place is like with a menorah;[816] fifty-three is the year Mr. Benes says we took care of business in Guatemala[817]/how many years ago Uncle Leo stiffed Mrs. Seinfeld;[818] fifty-two is the street where you will find Lactose Intolerants Anonymous;[819] fifty-one is the percentage of turns that are right turns;[820] fifty is how many feet out the Great Beast was[821]/the bet to walk off with an egg roll[822]/how much Uncle Leo owes Mrs. Seinfeld[823]/how many dollars Jerry was willing to pay for the marble rye[824]/how much Newman paid Kramer for Elaine's bike[825]/how much a Jackhammer rental is[826]/How much money

[810] S02E02, "The Pony Remark," written by Larry David, Jerry Seinfeld.

[811] S03E09, "The Nose Job," written by Peter Mehlman.

[812] S04E20, "The Junior Mint," written by Andy Robin.

[813] S07E10, "The Gum," written by Tom Gammill, Max Pross.

[814] S09E19, "The Maid," written by Alec Berg, David Mandel, Jeff Schaffer, Kit Boss, Peter Mehlman.

[815] S07E21/22, "The Bottle Deposit," written by Gregg Kavet, Andy Robin.

[816] S09E10, "The Strike," written by Dan O'Keefe, Alec Berg, Jeff Schaffer.

[817] S02E03, "The Jacket," written by Larry David, Jerry Seinfeld.

[818] S06E17, "The Kiss Hello," written by Larry David, Jerry Seinfeld.

[819] S02E04, "The Phone Message," written by Larry David, Jerry Seinfeld.

[820] S07E21/22, "The Bottle Deposit," written by Gregg Kavet, Andy Robin.

[821] S05E14, "The Marine Biologist," written by Ron Hauge, Charlie Rubin.

[822] S02E11, "The Chinese Restaurant," written by Larry David, Jerry Seinfeld.

[823] S06E17, "The Kiss Hello," written by Larry David, Jerry Seinfeld.

[824] S07E11, "The Rye," written by Carol Leifer.

[825] S07E13, "The Seven," written by Alec Berg, Jeff Schaffer.

[826] S08E16, "The Pothole," written by Steve O'Donnell, Dan O'Keefe.

Jerry's folks sent him because he bounced a check,[827] forty-nine are the pairs of sneakers Jerry wore/the cents a pound that cantaloupes are[828]/the number of Kramer's birthday wishes Newman deals for;[829] forty-eight are the baseball references; forty-seven are the number of George's girlfriends/the order number for Elaine's Supreme Flounder;[830] forty-six are the food items mentioned/the year the beltless trench coat was invented[831]/where the Pakistani restaurant is that Mr. Benes likes;[832] forty-five are the minutes it takes Morty to fill out a form[833]/the cost of testing food for fat content;[834] forty-four are the Newman appearances; forty-three is the street where you can find the Soup Nazi;[835] forty-two is the size of Bania's new suit[836]/the page number of the cartoon;[837] forty-one is the volume of TV Guide that Frank is missing;[838] forty is how many pairs of underwear George has[839]/Jerry's suit size[840]/the number of times the main characters watch TV; thirty-nine are the years that George enjoyed his milk products;[841] thirty-eight are the years Morty sold raincoats[842]/what the healer charges, in dollars;[843] thirty-seven are the times Elaine thinks she Did That

[827] S08E11, "The Little Jerry," written by Jennifer Crittenden.
[828] S02E01, "The Ex-Girlfriend," written by Larry David, Jerry Seinfeld.
[829] S09E08, "The Betrayal," written by David Mandel, Peter Mehlman.
[830] S08E16, "The Pothole," written by Steve O'Donnell, Dan O'Keefe.
[831] S05E18/19, "The Raincoats," written by Tom Gammill, Max Pross, Larry David, Jerry Seinfeld.
[832] S02E03, "The Jacket," written by Larry David, Jerry Seinfeld.
[833] S04E05, "The Wallet," written by Larry David.
[834] S05E07, "The Non-Fat Yogurt," written by Larry David.
[835] S07E06, "The Soup Nazi," written by Spike Feresten.
[836] S06E07, "The Soup," written by Fred Stoller.
[837] S09E13, "The Cartoon," written by Bruce Eric Kaplan.
[838] S05E10, "The Cigar Store Indian," written by Tom Gammill, Max Pross.
[839] S02E04, "The Phone Message," written by Larry David, Jerry Seinfeld.
[840] S06E07, "The Soup," written by Fred Stoller.
[841] S02E04, "The Phone Message," written by Larry David, Jerry Seinfeld.
[842] S05E18/19, "The Raincoats," written by Tom Gammill, Max Pross, Larry David, Jerry Seinfeld.
[843] S02E08, "The Heart Attack," written by Larry Charles.

with Jerry[844]/the street in Queens where the Costanzas live/the year of King Edward VIII's wedding cake;[845] thirty-six is how old Jerry is when he is stranded;[846] thirty-five are the geriatrics throwing elbows[847]/the percent Kramer wants in the raincoat business;[848] thirty-four is the street where Mendy's is located; thirty-three are the discs in the box set/the age when George has not yet reached puberty;[849] thirty-two are the Superhero references; thirty-one is the size Jerry changes his jeans to;[850] thirty are hours that a sponge is worthy[851]/hours that are lost in the fjord;[852] twenty-nine are the Susan Ross appearances/the June 1980 day Jerry's vomit streak started;[853] twenty-eight are the scenes in a doctor's office or hospital/how much it would cost to rub out two cats[854]/how many times George puts on or removes his glasses; twenty-seven are the appearances by Estelle Costanza/how many shower minutes Kramer whittled down to, from an hour;[855] twenty-six are the Chinese food references/the mentions of shrinkage/the mentions of Festivus; twenty-five are the times Jerry thinks he Did That with Elaine[856]/the minutes per day Morty uses his exercise device[857]/the percent Kramer gets in the raincoat business[858]/how much Frank's life is

[844] S02E09, "The Deal," written by Larry David.

[845] S09E18, "The Frogger," written by Gregg Kavet, Andy Robin, Steve Koren, Dan O'Keefe.

[846] S03E10, "The Stranded," written by Larry David, Jerry Seinfeld, Matt Goldman.

[847] S08E18, "The Nap," written by Gregg Kavet, Andy Robin.

[848] S05E18/19, "The Raincoats," written by Tom Gammill, Max Pross, Larry David, Jerry Seinfeld.

[849] S02E08, "The Heart Attack," written by Larry Charles.

[850] S07E09, "The Sponge," written by Peter Mehlman.

[851] Ibid.

[852] S07E05, "The Hot Tub," written by Gregg Kavet, Andy Robin.

[853] S05E13, "The Dinner Party," written by Larry David.

[854] S01E05, "The Stock Tip," written by Larry David, Jerry Seinfeld.

[855] S09E09, "The Apology," written by Jennifer Crittenden.

[856] S02E09, "The Deal," written by Larry David.

[857] S08E12, "The Money," written by Peter Mehlman.

[858] S05E18/19, "The Raincoats," written by Tom Gammill, Max Pross, Larry David, Jerry Seinfeld.

worth to George;[859] twenty-four are the times Elaine belly laughs/how much it costs to rent a car in Florida[860]/minutes it took George to get from 81st to JFK;[861] twenty-three are the amount of bad subs Elaine had to eat[862]/the date, in December, of Festivus[863]/the length, in hours, of Elaine's plane ride[864]/where George parked the car, in the purple section;[865] twenty-two are the fictional movies; twenty-one are the years it took for actual Muffin Tops to hit the market[866]/the times Jerry says, "Yeah come on up."; twenty is the denomination that gets defaced and thrown out a window[867]/the appearances by J. Peterman/the dollar amount Kramer gets by being greeted with "Hey."[868]/how many lies George is living[869]/How many years of buffer Jerry got before his parents moved in[870]/the MPH over which Morty Seinfeld will never drive;[871] nineteen are the cigars smoked by Kramer; eighteen are the scenes at an airport or on a plane/the amount, thousands, that Kramer won on Papa Nick;[872] seventeen is the stage number upon which the show was filmed/the age at which Kramer ran away to Sweden[873]/Keith Hernandez's uniform number;[874] sixteen are the number of "Hello, Newman!"s/the number of Kramer's

[859] S05E18/19, "The Raincoats," written by Tom Gammill, Max Pross, Larry David, Jerry Seinfeld.

[860] S03E03, "The Pen," written by Larry David.

[861] S04E07, "The Bubble Boy," written by Larry David, Larry Charles.

[862] S09E10, "The Strike," written by Dan O'Keefe, Alec Berg, Jeff Schaffer.

[863] Ibid.

[864] S09E08, "The Betrayal," written by David Mandel, Peter Mehlman.

[865] S03E06, "The Parking Garage," written by Larry David.

[866] S08E21, "The Muffin Tops," written by Spike Feresten.

[867] S05E22, "The Opposite," written by Andy Cowan, Larry David, Jerry Seinfeld.

[868] S07E24, "The Invitations," written by Larry David.

[869] S06E13, "The Scofflaw," written by Peter Mehlman.

[870] S07E16, "The Shower Head," written by Peter Mehlman, Marjorie Gross.

[871] S09E15, "The Wizard," written by Steve Lookner.

[872] S03E13, "The Subway," written by Larry Charles.

[873] S03E21, "The Letter," written by Larry David.

[874] S03E17/18, "The Boyfriend," written by Larry David, Larry Levin.

girlfriends; fifteen is the stareable age when something comes across your field of vision[875]/appearances by Uncle Leo/Larry David cameos/Golden Globe nominations/minutes George *says* it took to get from 81st to JFK;[876] fourteen are the years of Jerry's vomit streak[877]/the number of jobs George had/the years Morty was in Red Chinese prison;[878] thirteen are the "Get out!" shoves from Elaine/the bowls of cereal eaten/how long a date would last, in seconds if you could say whatever you wanted; twelve are the average amount of cereals in Jerry's kitchen/the years Kramer was on strike/uses of "Yada yada"; eleven is how many minutes Elaine needs to clear her head; ten are the Emmy awards/the Kennedy references/times George says he can't believe this/ten are how many seconds it takes for Kramer to fix Elaine's neck/the minutes Jerry or Elaine spend in the shower; nine are the years on the air/Jerry's favorite number/the multi-part episodes; eight is the number on Puddy's jacket/the number of subway rides/the dollars stolen from George's wallet/how many previous plans there were from outer space/how many Pottery Barn catalogues Kramer got in one month/the Van Buren Boys' gang sign/how many dollars Kramer paid for Newman's bunion stories; Seven is the perfect baby name/the dates that qualify for a face-to-face breakup/the pounds Elaine gained from the non-fat yogurt; six is the maximum percentage of people who are datable/the cost of a marble rye/the length of Newman's birthday wish hot streak; five is the floor Jerry, Kramer, and Newman lived on/the Art Vandelay references/for how many cents you could once get a Hershey/the minutes Elaine begs strangers to drive around the garage; four are the reservations at the restaurant/The Three Stooges references/the time

[875] S04E16, "The Shoes," written by Larry David, Jerry Seinfeld.
[876] S04E07, "The Bubble Boy," written by Larry David, Larry Charles.
[877] S05E13, "The Dinner Party," written by Larry David.
[878] S03E06, "The Parking Garage," written by Larry David.

George Did That in an inappropriate place; three is the number of days it takes George to learn Portuguese/the pints of blood Kramer donates to Jerry/the Desperate Housewives Jerry dated/the toilet paper squares Elaine asks for/stipulations of "The Deal"/ how many months the Summer of George lasted/the cost, in dollars, of a gryo at Queenboro Plaza/how many cannolis per week Newman requires/how many years George was stuck on Weebolos 'cause he kept losing the Pinewood Derby; two are real and they are spectacular; one is the rating when Seinfeld went off the air; nothing is what happened.

No, no, no, nothing happened!

Who knows one hundred and six? I sure don't know one hundred and six. I could not find anything meaningful aside from the 106th episode – The Doodle.[879] There wasn't even a production code 106, because the first season was only five episodes. So it ends here, and I think it's safe to say:

Well, something happened.[880]

---

[879] S06E20, "The Doodle," written by Alec Berg, Jeff Schaffer.
[880] S04E03, "The Pitch," written by Larry David.

One Pilot

The Chronicles of Seinfeld[881]

One pilot, one pilot that NBC bought for bupkiss. One pilot, one pilot.

Then came nearly a year of silence before they cancelled a Bob Hope special so they could find money to produce four more episodes, following the "Chronicles" show that they bought for bupkiss. One pilot, one pilot.

Then they ordered a second season of twelve episodes because it showed a bit of promise, despite nobody really getting what the show was about (it was about nothing, duh), following the flier they took on the first season and episode, which everyone hated, which they bought for bupkiss. One pilot, one pilot.

Then came season #3, and its season was a full complement of 24 episodes (actually, 23; what is the deal with that?), and had several bold[882] and daring[883] episodes, and Jerry's powers grew more powerful under the yellow sun, and the show won its first ever writing emmy,[884] with more to come, and this, after a measly season #2 of twelve episodes, following a whole season of just five (actually, one plus four), following that long layoff after the first episode, which producers said "Stunk," which NBC bought for bupkiss. One pilot, one pilot.

---

[881] S01E01, "The Seinfeld Chronicles," written by Larry David, Jerry Seinfeld.
[882] S03E06, "The Parking Garage," written by Larry David.
[883] S03E10, "The Stranded," written by Larry David, Jerry Seinfeld, Matt Goldman.
[884] Outstanding Writing in a Comedy Series, Elaine Pope, Larry Charles, "The Fix-Up."

Then came season #4, which included absolute classics,[885] and the show climbed into the top 25 in ratings, and won its first acting[886] and series[887] emmys, following a stellar season #3, which came on the heels of the measly season #2, and all this after the poor showing of the first season, which NBC bought for bupkiss. One pilot, one pilot.

Then came season #5, which continued to build momentum, as Richards won another acting emmy, and as it finished third for the year in ratings, following its slow but steady climb in season #4, built on the critical success, but medicore ratings performance of season #3, which somehow built on the middling ratings of season #2, which was built on the fluff of season #1, which NBC bought for bupkiss. One pilot, one pilot.

Then came season #6, and the show hit #1 in the ratings for the first time, after the great build-up from season #5, following a nice season #4, a good #3, a piddling #2, and blah #1. I mean, they started (and finished!) with talking about shirt buttons, which NBC bought for bupkiss. One pilot, one pilot.

Then came season #7, and Louis-Dreyfus won her first of 367 (kind of, just kind of,[888] an underexaggeration) career emmys,[889] as the show slipped in rank to #2, but gained in ratings to 21.2. Go figure. This after a great season #6, awards-filled season #5,[890] brave episodes in season #4,[891] meh season #3, eh season #2, and beh #1, which NBC bought for bupkiss. One pilot, one pilot.

---

[885] S04E11, "The Contest," written by Larry David.
[886] Outstanding Supporting Actor in a Comedy Series, Michael Richards.
[887] Outstanding Comedy Series. It would never win again, thanks to Frasier (shakes fist angrily).
[888] S03E16, "The Fix-Up," written by Larry Charles, Elaine Pope.
[889] Outstanding Supporting Actress in a Comedy Series, Julia Louis-Dreyfus.
[890] Three Golden Globes, a Writers Guild of America Award, and an ASCAP.
[891] S04E07, "The Bubble Boy," written by Larry David, Larry Charles.

Then came season #8, with another Richards emmy, and Seinfeld took over as showrunner from David, retired the stand-up parts, and moved up the pace, but ratings remained strong, building on season #7, #6, #5, #4, #3, #2, and #1. Look at me, I can count, which NBC bought for bupkiss. One pilot, one pilot.

Then came season #9, where the writers went madcap[892] and bonkers,[893] but the show left while on top, with Seinfeld claiming it was because 9 is his favorite number, thereby turning down a shocking $110 million. In summary, season #8 was a turn to a new direction,[894] season #7 was a bit wayward,[895] season #6 was super-successful, season #5 was the much-acclaimed hump-series, season #4 was the most self-referential thing ever,[896] season #3 was bravery,[897] if you ask me, season #2 laid the base, season #1 was majorly exploratory,[898] then it went wee wee wee, all the way into syndication. And all this because NBC bought for bupkiss. One pilot, one pilot.

---

[892] S09E08, "The Betrayal," written by David Mandel, Peter Mehlman.
[893] S09E06, "The Merv Griffin Show," written by Bruce Eric Kaplan.
[894] S08E21, "The Muffin Tops," written by Spike Feresten.
[895] S07E14/15, "The Cadillac," written by Larry David, Jerry Seinfeld.
[896] S04E23/24, "The Pilot," written by Larry David.
[897] S03E15, "The Suicide," written by Tom Leopold.
[898] S01E02, "The Stake Out," written by Larry David, Jerry Seinfeld.

About the Author

Young Guy, He's Got a New Book Coming Out, and It's About[899]

Martin has been writing freelance for more than 20 years, mostly on Jewish interest topics. He is the co-creator of a popular Jewish news satire website called TheKnish.com. His work has been published in The Huffington Post, The Denver Post, The Washington Times, The Jewish Press, Country Yossi Magazine, Modern Magazine, The Jewish Link, bangitout.com, scoogiespin.com, jewcentral.com, and israelinsider.com. His work has also been translated for Germany's only weekly Jewish newspaper, The Judische Allgemeine. He is currently the beat reporter for JRunnersClub.org and the surname columnist for jewishworldreview.com.

The Emoji Haggadah, his sixth book, generated much praise, and was covered in The Jewish Week, The Jewish Link of NJ, Jewish Vues, Vos Iz Neias, Jewish Book Council, NorthJersey.com, The Forward, Jewish Journal, J-Wire, Vox, The Jewish Press, The Judische Allgemeine, and various blogs.

This is his seventh book. He'll eat it up, he loves it so.

---

899 S05E22, "The Opposite," written by Andy Cowan, Larry David, Jerry Seinfeld.

The author, Purim, circa last millennium.

CPSIA information can be obtained
at www.ICGtesting.com
Printed in the USA
BVHW032128250320
576030BV00001B/31